Across the Water

Teaching Irish Music and Dance at Home and Abroad

Rebecca E. Farrell

Published in partnership with
MENC: The National Association for Music Education

ROWMAN & LITTLEFIELD EDUCATION
A division of
ROWMAN & LITTLEFIELD PUBLISHERS, INC.
Lanham • New York • Toronto • Plymouth, UK

Published in partnership with MENC: The National Association for Music Education

Published by Rowman & Littlefield Education
A division of Rowman & Littlefield Publishers, Inc.
A wholly owned subsidary of The Rowman & Littlefield Publishing Group, Inc.
4501 Forbes Boulevard, Suite 200, Lanham, Maryland 20706
http://www.rowmaneducation.com

Estover Road, Plymouth PL6 7PY, United Kingdom

British Library Cataloguing in Publication Information Available

Library of Congress Cataloging-in-Publication Data

Farrell, Rebecca E., 1980–
  Across the water : teaching Irish music and dance at home and abroad / Rebecca E. Farrell.
    p. cm.
  "Published in partnership with MENC: The National Association for Music Education."
  Includes bibliographical references.
  ISBN 978-1-60709-577-4 (cloth : alk. paper)—ISBN 978-1-60709-578-1 (pbk. : alk. paper)— ISBN 978-1-60709-579-8 (electronic)
  1. Folk music—Ireland—Instruction and study. 2. Folk music—Instruction and study—Ireland. 3. Folk music—Instruction and study—United States. 4. Folk dancing, Irish—Study and teaching—Ireland. 5. Folk dancing, Irish—Study and teaching—United States. I. Title.
  ML3654.F36 2010
  781.62'91620071—dc22

                                                                    2010017828

∞ ™ The paper used in this publication meets the minimum requirements of American National Standard for Information Sciences—Permanence of Paper for Printed Library Materials, ANSI/NISO Z39.48-1992.

Printed in the United States of America

It seems to me that for those who have ears to hear, this music of ours possesses the power of magic: it can put us in touch with ourselves in ways no other Irish art form can do. It can touch the pulse of ancestral memory, allowing us to redefine our dreams of what it is to be Irish. It can bring the lonely famine landscape to life, it can soothe the trauma and trouble of existence, it is possessed of the veiled eroticism of tenderness. It can adorn a moment of joy, it can sharpen a moment of sorrow. It is a gift of nature, dispensed with the abandon of wild flowers.

—Tony McMahon, "Music of the Powerful and Majestic Past"

Contents

Illustration and Tables

FIGURES

PHOTOS

TABLES

CD Tracks

(Listening Examples)

1. "My Aunt Jane"
2. "Óró Sé Do Bheatha 'Bhaile"
3. "The Fox and the Hare"
4. "An Maidrín Rua" ("The Little Fox")
5. "Believe Me If All Those Endearing Young Charms"
6. "I Am the Master"/"Dusty Bluebells"
7. Wexford Carol
8. Basic "Milltown Jig"
9. Ornamented "Milltown Jig"
10. Ornamentation Demonstration: Cut
11. Ornamentation Demonstration: Roll
12. Ornamentation Demonstration: Short Roll

Vocals: Rebecca E. Farrell
Tin whistle: Norah Rendell
Sound engineer: Niall Keegan
All listening examples were recorded at the University of Limerick in June 2006.

Preface

Music educators and ethnomusicologists alike are fascinated with "the other." By studying "the other" we are able to learn not only about a culture we had previously been unexposed to but about ourselves as well. When traveling into the unknown, it is important to examine the method of transmission used by the people raised within that community to pass on their language, traditions, and music. Although an ethnomusicologist's and music educator's purposes for looking at the method of transmission are different, their common interest in cultures from around the world indicates that there is a point where the two disciplines coexist. It is at this point where I began my research in September 2005.

For music educators, the journey into "the other" develops out of a desire to introduce their students to ethnic groups other than their own. It is from this exploration that teachers hope children will learn how to respect and embrace differences as they grow to adulthood. For the ethnomusicologist the study of "the other" helps the researcher learn about him- or herself. It is the putting of the "I" into the ethnography that allows field researchers to gain a better understanding of what it means to be a member of the new community as well as their own.

My research, as an ethnomusicologist and a music educator, has focused on an issue in applied ethnomusicology where music education is a principal concern. By studying how traditional Irish music is taught in a variety of classroom settings in Ireland, I have attained a firmer understanding of how to "pass it on" to my students in the United States. It is my hope that the research I completed at the University of Limerick will be used by other educators to introduce traditional Irish music to their students.

Water metaphors are commonly used in Irish traditional music and dance to refer to the great distances that separate loved ones, the desire to erase past wrongs, and the hope for a better future. On one level in this study, water is used to symbolize the tendency of music educators to look to the native soil for guidance when teaching the culture in its diasporic setting. On another level the water imagery is used to symbolize the two separate disciplines of music education and ethnomusicology and the resources and knowledge each has to offer the other. It is my hope that this book demonstrates the work that can be produced when these two disciplines coexist and bridge that watery divide.

Acknowledgments

I would like to take this opportunity to thank several people who were integral to the completion of this book. First of all, I would like to thank the faculty and staff at the Irish World Academy of Music and Dance (University of Limerick) for accepting me into the ethnomusicology master's program and then assisting me throughout the entire thesis process. Thank you to Niall Keegan, Sandra Joyce, Dr. John O'Flynn, Norah Rendell, Denis Liddy, Ina Fitzpatrick, and Michelle Mulcahy for sharing their knowledge and talents with me. I wouldn't have been able to produce this book without their help.

Also, I would like to express my appreciation to my colleagues and the administration at Palmyra-Macedon Central School District for their willingness to let me leave for a year to chase a lifelong dream. I am very fortunate to belong to a district that believes in supporting lifelong learning.

In addition, I would like to thank my family, my fellow ethnomusicology classmates, and my friends both "at home and abroad" for their support throughout the original thesis process and then again as I transitioned this work from thesis to book.

Most of all I would like to thank my husband, Brian, who believed this book could become a reality long before I did. Thank you for your editing expertise, Photoshop skills, and never-ending support for my love of everything Irish.

This book is dedicated to my family, who has always believed that with a lot of hard work and a little faith, anything is possible.

1

When Theory Meets Practice: The Application of Ethnomusicological Methods in the Classroom

The issue of musical transmission is pivotal for all American educators who are attempting to create a world music curriculum. Since many preservice music education programs in the United States emphasize the classical method of teaching music by note, a beginning teacher is often unsure of how to proceed when integrating other cultures into units of study. For those men and women the question becomes what teaching approach should be used to introduce unfamiliar songs and cultures to students in a manner that is both appropriate and accurate.

To answer this question, three topics need to be addressed. First, research in ethnomusicology must be surveyed, and the effect that information can have on how accurately music is transmitted in the music classroom must be assessed. To accomplish this I will review two ethnomusicology-based texts, Bruno Nettl et al.'s *Excursions in World Music* and Jeff Todd Titon's *Worlds of Music*, and examine their ability to serve as the theoretical background for a world music curriculum.

Second, an overview of a few key resources available to practicing teachers, including several works by Patricia Shehan Campbell, is necessary to illustrate the methods currently used by leading music educators to integrate the world's cultures into the classroom. Finally, the intersection between theory and practice, or ethnomusicology and music education, and the resources that are produced as a result of this intersection will be addressed. In particular Barbara Lundquist and C. K. Szego's *Musics of the World's Cultures: A Source Book for Music Educators* will be looked at as representative of what is possible when the methods of ethnomusicology are put to use in the classroom.

As the information age continues to boom and the world becomes smaller by the day, world music is developing into an increasingly important element of every general and instrumental music curriculum. Ethnomusicology can provide the music education field with a wealth of knowledge about how music is used by the world's cultures and how it should be transmitted to nonnative people in a respectful and representative manner. By reaching out to ethnomusicology, music educators can enhance their own practice in both the classroom and wider musical community.

ETHNOMUSICOLOGY AND
ITS INFLUENCE ON MUSIC EDUCATION

Ethnomusicology has the power to create a revolution in the world of music and education if it follows the implication of its discoveries and develops as a method and not merely an area of study.

—John Blacking (2000, p. 4)

According to Bruno Nettl, ethnomusicology can be used "to find ways of comprehending an entire musical culture, identifying its central paradigms and finding points of entry, or perhaps handles, for grasping a culture or capturing a music" (Nettl, 1995). With the help of Charles Capwell, Philip V. Bohlman, Isabel K. F. Wong, and Thomas Turino, Nettl attempts to achieve this goal in all four editions of *Excursions in World Music*. (There is a fifth edition of *Excursions in World Music* that has been released since my original research. It was not reviewed in this book.) For example, the most recently released edition introduces the reader to a world of music while emphasizing the uniqueness and diversity of each culture. The authors hope to persuade the reader to listen to music of cultures other than his or her own by providing the student or music educator with a picture of the way the world's people make music, think about it, use it in their lives, structure and perform it (Nettl et al., 2003).

Each chapter, written by a practicing ethnomusicologist, begins by focusing on a detailed description of a musical event that broadly represents the cultural area. Following this example, the music culture is described as it exists currently, with information about the history of the ethnic group and description of musical life, ideas of music, and of musical style and instruments. Finally, there is a brief explanation of a few additional musical genres or cultural contexts where music can be found within the community and a consideration of recent developments and popular music (Nettl et al., 2003). Complete with pictures and descriptions of native instruments and representative recordings of each culture, this textbook can provide music educators with the theoretical and cultural basis for world music units in the classroom. Since many of the world's cultures transmit their music orally from one generation to the next, it is appropriate for the music educator to learn a piece from the recording aurally and then teach it to his or her students in a similar manner. Unfortunately, translations of the song texts included on the accompanying recording have not been provided by the authors, and as a result, actual repertoire for units on cultures such as Native Americans might be best found from other sources.

Although Jeff Todd Titon's textbook *Worlds of Music* is constructed in a similar manner to *Excursions in World Music*, it includes the practical element that the other lacks. In an attempt to show that the world is a fluid and living place where history and the present intermingle daily, the chapter authors begin by describing the older musical layers of a given region, followed by increasingly more contemporary musical styles, forms, and attitudes. Within each section specific pieces representative of a culture are described and transcribed. Also, maps and pictures taken in the field are included in the discussion of each region, and, most importantly, a few chapters even contain diagrams on how to re-create culturally significant instruments (Titon, 1996). Using these diagrams as a guide, music educators can build instruments from a variety of world cultures with their students, and then use the finished products to create music representative of the people being studied. While having the authentic instruments in class is always the ideal situation, the time spent constructing the instruments by hand provides teachers with an opportunity to discuss the role instruments play in society, as well as the status of an instrument maker and musician in the culture.

While all the chapters would be useful in the creation of authentic and appropriate cultural units, the last chapter in *Worlds of Music* could attract many students to the study of music at the high school level. In this section David B. Reck, Mark Slobin, and Jeff Todd Titon outline how an individual music student, much in the manner of a practicing ethnomusicologist, could discover and document music he or she is interested in. This type of project, complete with an ethnography, field recordings, and photographic essays, could be a great alternative to the standard written recall exam given at the completion of many mandatory "Music in Our Lives" courses. By facilitating this type of project, music educators could help students "experience what it is like to be an ethnomusicologist puzzling out his or her way toward understanding an unfamiliar music" (Titon, 1996, p. 518). Also, this type of fieldwork will help students begin to see music as a human expression that continues to grow and flourish throughout life. In reality this is what music educators hope to achieve by introducing world music into their classrooms. Although both Nettl's and Titon's texts are thought provoking and can be useful to some degree to a music educator, *Worlds of Music* provides teachers with the tools to accurately and authentically transmit several cultures from around the world to their students.

MUSIC EDUCATION AND THE TRANSMISSION
OF WORLD MUSIC IN THE CLASSROOM

> In the international age, we must seek to understand the perspectives of people from every part of the globe. Cultures and countries are increasingly interdependent in economic and political matters. Our survival as a world community may depend on our ability to understand the similarities that bind and the differences that distinguish us as subsets of the human species.
>
> —Patricia Shehan Campbell (Anderson & Campbell, 1996, p. viii)

When music educators gather to discuss multicultural music education, one name is always included. Patricia Shehan Campbell, a distinguished professor at the University of Washington in Seattle, has dedicated her professional career to the study of world music and its application to the general music classroom. Her influence on the methods used by current music educators to teach world music to their students is astounding and has not been equaled by any other in the field. A representative sample of her incredible body of work will be addressed in this section of the chapter.

As with all her textbooks, *Lessons from the World: A Cross-Cultural Guide to Music Teaching and Learning* begins with an examination of a concept and then is followed by recommendations for the application of techniques to classrooms and studios. Drawing upon the research of ethnomusicologists such as Alan Merriam and John Blacking, Dr. Campbell "examines the importance of ear training and improvisation in the history of European art music, in a sampling of world cultures and in the making of young musicians in contemporary education settings" (1991, p. xii). The emphasis given in the book to the aural and creative components of music teaching and learning is meant to impress upon the reader the importance of these aspects as a part of a shared human phenomenon. Campbell's statement distinctly reminds one of John Blacking's discussions of humanly organized sound in *How Musical Is Man?* and aptly displays the influence that ethnomusicological research has had on the field of music education (Campbell, 1991, p. xiii).

While this textbook does not directly provide a music educator with resources that could be used in the construction of cultural units, it does remind him or her that many of the techniques used in the transmission of Western art music, such as mnemonic devices, musical metaphors, and use of vocalization, are common throughout the world. It also provides teachers with a framework to begin their own observations of new cultures, emphasizing the importance of studying the role of enculturation, training, and formal schooling within the ethnic community as indicators of the wider cultural music values. Finally, it supplies musicians both in the classroom and in the studio with exercises and experiences to strengthen the listening, performing, and improvising skills of their students. This knowledge will in turn provide students with the tools to be able to one day absorb music from other cultures in the same manner as those within the society.

Following *Lessons from the World*, Dr. Campbell coauthored a book called *Roots and Branches* with Ellen McCullough-Brabson and Judith Cook Tucker. Specifically for elementary school children, this book introduced music educators to songs and games from around the world. The songs are set in their cultural context, and each chapter contains a sketch of geographic, cultural, economic, and historical factors at the appropriate cognitive level, a map of the country and surrounding areas, and a brief biography and photograph of the song contributor (Campbell et al., 1994). In addition to these elements, what makes this book unique and still a very useful multicultural resource fifteen years later is that the authors encourage the teacher to learn the song by rote and not by the simple transcribed score included in the book. At the time this resource was written, oral transmission of a song or dance would not have been considered as important as it is today. Also, the positioning of the music in its cultural context illustrates the respect Campbell and her colleagues have for cultures other than their own and the frequency with which music educators who wish to transmit music from around the world to their students should use this resource.

In 1989 Campbell collaborated with William M. Anderson and several other experts in the field of world music to publish *Multicultural Perspectives in Music Education*, followed by a second edition in 1996. Like Bruno Nettl et al.'s *Excursions in World Music*, *Multicultural Perspectives in Music Education* describes a variety of world cultures and then, taking the idea one step further, provides music educators with a collection of lessons and lesson models that can be used to integrate world music within the full expanse of the school curriculum. In addition to these elements, Dr. Campbell and Dr. Anderson throughout the book implore teachers to create an educational philosophy that recognizes the many cultural contributions made by different people. It is the opinion of the authors that students will not be able to learn from a multicultural perspective if this foundation is not in place (Anderson & Campbell, 1996). Finally, the book provides beginning educators with instructional approaches and teaching tools that can be used to accurately integrate world music into their classroom.

If preservice music education programs begin to consistently provide their students with resources like *Multicultural Perspectives in Music Education* and the recently developed Global Music Series, coedited by Bonnie Wade and Patricia Shehan Campbell, then new teachers will be able to realistically represent many cultures from around the world with minimal anxiety.

WHEN THEORY MEETS PRACTICE: MUSIC EDUCATION AND ETHNOMUSICOLOGY PARTNERSHIPS

For a student to learn Western, Indian, Zairian or Japanese music without seeing how each one fits into a context of world music is somewhat like teaching the geography of France or Zaire or India or Japan without the use of a globe.

—Bruno Nettl (Lundquist & Szego, 1998, p. 23)

Over the last several decades music educators have begun to reach out to the ethnomusicology community for help creating texts and partnerships that will provide teachers with quality and appropriate music from a variety of cultures. *Musics of the World's Cultures: A Source Book for Music Educators* is representative of these efforts. Published by the International Society for Music Education (ISME), this book seeks to illustrate ISME's position on the use of cultural music in music education, the three separate perspectives (ethnomusicological, performance, and music education) on musics of the world's cultures in music education, representative case studies of how this music is being used by practicing teachers, and an extensive list of resources.

Along with several other ethnomusicologists, Bruno Nettl is a major contributor to this sourcebook. In his chapter titled "An Ethnomusicological Perspective," he introduces music educators to the purpose of ethnomusicology and explains that the "people in ethnomusicology are the ones responsible for making world music available to educators, academics and performers" (Nettl, 1998, p. 23). Throughout his contribution to the sourcebook, Nettl encourages teachers to create units that study all of the musics of a culture instead of only the most traditional. By examining where the traditional intermingles with the contemporary (e.g., church and school) teachers can help students understand how cultural changes affect the music of a people. Also, Nettl's discussion on critiquing a musical performance using the terms contained in the culture's aesthetic standards presents an interesting topic for conversation among students studying in a multicultural setting (Nettl, 1998). If students from another culture are taught how different societies of the world evaluate their music, does this give them the right, as outsiders, to evaluate music of those cultures using native methods? This question could provide a teacher with an interesting basis for a class discussion at any age level about respect for others.

Finally, Nettl stresses that an ethnomusicologist or music educator will have a greater appreciation of music from other heritages if he or she has a clear understanding of the method one's own culture uses to structure and integrate music into everyday life (Nettl, 1998). Quite frequently in today's politically correct world, music educators are so eager to represent cultures from outside their own country that they forget the importance of studying their own. It is from our understanding of our own roots that the branches of understanding others may grow. I feel this reminder is Nettl's most important contribution to the *Music of the World's Cultures: A Source Book for Music Educators*.

Barbara Lundquist follows Nettl's perspective with the practicality of a seasoned music educator. Focused on the formation of a world music curriculum, she outlines decisions that need to be made prior to the creation of the units and elements that should be found in every cultural lesson. This includes clearly outlining the potential importance of each unit to the students as well as to the teachers themselves and creating a learning sequence that develops from experience and exposure to greater meaning (Lundquist & Szego, 1998). She also emphasizes the importance of teaching what the culture values musically and when possible bringing in an expert in the tradition to lead the class in a workshop. Ideally, these master classes would culminate in a short performance for the rest of the school so that the knowledge obtained throughout the day could be passed on to those not present (Lundquist & Szego, 1998).

Finally, in an effort to give music educators the concrete examples that they crave, the authors of *Musics of the World's Cultures: A Source Book for Music Educators* provide an essay on a multicultural program in existence at the San Francisco School in San Francisco, California. In this essay the development, philosophical underpinnings, celebration calendar, and construction of the entire program are discussed and broken down in a manner that clearly defines what must occur in order for a music curriculum like it to exist. Although it may not be the best example of the possibilities that can exist when multiculturalism is the foundation of a music program, it does provide a starting point for all educators who would like to turn their current aspirations into a reality.

As educators we are so trained to read and absorb every book and periodical on our subject that we often forget to look beyond what is written to what is currently happening in our community. At this point in this literature review it is crucial that the real-life partnerships between ethnomusicology, community music, and music education be cited for their importance to all areas of musical study. In this book community music will be defined as all musical activities that occur outside the formal music education settings. The International Society of Music Education (ISME) created a commission on Community Music Activity in 1982. Its mission is to "facilitate the exchange of information on areas relevant to the field of community music, encourage debate and dialogue on different international perspectives on community music and on current issues within the field, and where possible enter into dialogue with musicians and music educators in related fields and disseminate research and other information" (International Society of Music Education, 2009).

While many of the publications produced as a result of this partnership between educators and community music practitioners stretch far beyond the realm of this study, it is important to highlight the depth of work that has been completed and the importance of this knowledge to music educators in all aspects of their career. For instance, Margarete Arroyo's paper on "Community music inside a school context, questions and challenges for the music education" directly addresses the difficulty that can occur when the norms of the community music culture do not coexist with the expectations of the formal school environment. This problem is inherent in most cultures, including Ireland, and will be discussed in a later chapter. The information in papers such as these can be extremely useful to any music educator who teaches in a culturally rich area and can be accessed on the ISME website and through its online publications link.

While the International Society of Music Education has created partnerships to understand how music education occurs around the world, the Society of Ethnomusicology (SEM) has developed an Ethnomusicology in the Schools Project designed to bring ethnomusicologists into the classroom. This section of the society was created with the recognition that "teaching world musics is an integral part of the preschool through postgraduate music curriculum" (http://webdb.iu.edu/sem/scripts/groups/sections/education/education_section.cfm, accessed August 14, 2009). In order to nurture, advocate, and promote intercultural music education and instruction throughout the preschool through postgraduate music curriculum, ethnomusicologists volunteer to teach at any level in schools in the area of the annual SEM conference. Oftentimes these partnerships continue long after the initial session, with the ethnomusicologists serving as a music consultant to the district. Such interactions have produced several papers on a variety of ethnomusicology/education–based topics, as well as research-based lesson plans created by ethnomusicologists in their field of expertise. These resources can be easily accessed on the Society of Ethnomusicology website and are extremely useful to a music educator who is creating world music units.

CONCLUSION

Since the 1950s, ethnomusicologists have been studying and recording cultures from around the world. Frequently it will take ethnomusicologists several years in the field before they feel they understand an ethnic group and its musical culture. Obviously, this type of intensive study is not possible in the music classroom, and instead music educators should use the research of those in the field of ethnomusicology to inform their decision of what music to include in the curriculum.

By introducing students to a few well-chosen pieces and providing repeated opportunities for students to learn the music and understand where those songs or games fit into the lives of the native culture, music educators will be able to create an environment where respect and appreciation for differences will flourish.

A Brief History of Ireland and Its Music

Long before much of the world was exposed to Irish music through the Riverdance phenomenon, the Irish people living both at home and abroad had developed their own unique traditional musical culture. By defining Irish music as traditional, it is implied that the music has a long history within the community and "has been handed down by word of mouth or by example from one generation to another without written instruction" (Guzzi, 2009). Throughout history the transmission of this culture has been greatly affected by those in political and religious power. As a result, Irish traditional music must be taught within its historical context. It is through this history that we can understand the meaning of the music to the people of Ireland and the many others located around the world that at one point called the country home.

CELTIC AND NORMAN HISTORY IN IRELAND

> It's not at all surprising that a nation whose language and culture was suppressed through centuries, should make music virtually the sole vehicle for its spirit, personality and aspiration.
>
> —John Waters, *Irish Times*, June 29, 1993 (Curtis, 1994, p. 7)

Today, the term "Celtic" is used in a variety of manners. It has been used to sell CDs and DVDs to a global market of listeners; it has been used in a catch phrase referring to the economic boom Ireland was enjoying until the world's recent financial troubles; and it has been used to label the six modern

Celtic nationalities: the Irish, Scottish, Manx, Welsh, Bretons, and Cornish. Regardless of whether these uses of the term are correct or not, historically the Celtic people's control of Ireland influenced the country's language and music for a great expanse of time.

The early Celts were an Indo-European group who ruled Ireland and the surrounding area for over one thousand years. While most of their history was not recorded, their culture and language still influences the island today (Hast & Scott, 2004). Early documentation confirms their presence on the island as early as 2000 BCE (Sawyers, 2000). The early Celts lived in small kingdoms called *tuathas* (pronounced "thoó a-haw"). By the fifth century CE, missionaries, like the famous St. Patrick, had brought Christianity to Ireland and established religious orders in the country, and documentation shows that psalms and other religious songs were sung (Sawyers, 2000). Over the next several centuries, Irish monasteries became centers for learning, writing, and music. Many of the religious orders also established professional schools of music and tutored students in the playing of the harp as an accompanying instrument for the voice (McCarthy, 1999).

The arrival of the Normans in Ireland in 1169 quelled the political turmoil that had developed among the provincial kings during the previous decade and established a cultural renaissance that lasted for over a century. The Anglo-Norman control extended for a twenty-mile radius around what is today Dublin. During this relatively peaceful era, the Normans adopted the Irish culture and began to intermarry with the native people. This joining of communities greatly affected Irish music, and it was around this time that love songs, like those of the French and Spanish tradition, were integrated into Irish music (Sawyers, 2000). Also during this time music was established as an essential part of Irish life. The Gaelic chieftains, who descended from the early Celts, cultivated traditional music through an extensive system of patronage. Bards and harpists were employed by the Irish aristocracy to compose and perform songs praising and documenting the accomplishments of the patron. Considered to be essential members of the Gaelic kings' courts, such bards would proudly pass their position in the household onto their sons when it was time for the older man to retire (Hast & Scott, 2004).

IRELAND'S YEARS OF OCCUPATION BY THE ENGLISH

This culture renaissance came to an abrupt end with the arrival of the English army and King Henry II in 1171. After a series of invasions, the Normans were forced out of Ireland and a dark time in the history of Irish music commenced (Sawyers, 2000). Although initially intrigued by the Irish bardic tradition, official English views of Irish culture became increasingly less tolerant as the years went by. In 1366 the English Crown passed the Statutes of Kilkenny, which was created to protect against "English who wore Irish costume and spoke Irish, against intermarriage and fosterage with the Irish enemies" (Hast & Scott, 2004, p. 23). When Queen Elizabeth assumed the English throne in 1558, she feared that the itinerant Irish poets and harpers were political spies and consequently continued to create repressive legislation against the native population during her reign (Hast & Scott, 2004).

In 1571 the Earl of Kildare was commissioned by Queen Elizabeth to execute all bards (trained professional poets that were employed by clan chiefs) and harpers "wherever found" and destroy their instruments. In addition, Elizabeth declared that the composing of Irish music was now illegal. The bards, who had once been highly regarded members of Irish society, were forced to either secretly continue the tradition or turn to another way of life to survive (Sawyers, 2000).

By 1590 the roots of rebellion began to stir in Ulster. Gaelic chieftains Hugh O'Neill and Hugh O'Donnell set aside years of family rivalry to join forces as protectors of the Irish Catholics and lead a successful military challenge against the Earl of Essex. For a brief moment the Irish were blessed with a glimpse of freedom. However, on Christmas Day in 1601, the Earl of Essex's successor, Lord Mountjoy, defeated the Hughs at one of the most well-documented events in Irish history, the Battle of Kinsale (Sawyers, 2000). Following their defeat, the Irish aristocracy was outlawed and a royal decree commonly referred to as "hang the harpers" was put in place to further eradicate the rich Irish musical tradition (Fleischmann, 1952).

Six years after the Christmas Day battle, Rory O'Donnell, the brother of the patriot Hugh O'Donnell, and ninety other Ulster chiefs went into voluntary exile and fled to mainland Europe. This departure, called the Flight of the Earls, was a major turning point in Irish history and also had dire effects on the country's culture (Sawyers, 2000). Within a century, half the land in Ulster was transferred to the Scottish and English colonists, and the native Irish were moved to less fertile lands (Shields & Gershen, 2000). The rule of the English commonwealth and invasion under Oliver Cromwell began in 1649 and worsened the already volatile situation. During Cromwell's rule, all wandering musicians were required to obtain letters from local authorities before being allowed to travel through their own country. Also, Cromwell evicted rebel leaders from their land, Catholic priests were outlawed, and the saying of Mass was forbidden (Sawyers, 2000). Songs like "Rocks of Bawn" were written to commiserate about the atrocities that were occurring at the time.

In 1685 the Catholic King James II assumed the English throne, and for three years the Irish were granted a reprieve. Unfortunately, in 1688, the Glorious Revolution brought William of Orange and his wife, Mary, to power, and another wave of oppression began. James and his army tried to march through Ulster to regain the throne, but they were badly beaten by William at the Battle of the Boyne. As a result, James fled to France. This ensured that the Protestants would flourish in Ulster and was the final defeat of the Catholic Gaelic Ireland. This battle has inspired many Protestant tunes, like "The Boyne Water," that are still sung today (Sawyers, 2000).

During the last ten years of the seventeenth century and into the early eighteenth century, the situation for Irish Catholics became increasingly dire. In 1691 the Treaty of Limerick forced the last of the Irish nobility to leave the country, and soon after that the notorious anti-Catholic Penal Laws were created. The Irish were forced to abandon Catholicism or surrender property and any chance of a decent education. This demand was a steep blow to a culture of people whose religion was the foundation of their music, language, and daily life. In order to practice their religion, people would meet in a remote part of the country at a large rock, which would serve as an altar, and hold open-air services. Songs like "Were You at the Rock" were written to recount this difficult period. In addition to these rules, Irish Catholics had to pay tithes to established Protestant churches and couldn't participate in any government service, teach, or purchase land (Sawyers, 2000).

During the eighteenth century the laws became less stringent, and as a result traditional and classical music began to be practiced with greater freedom once again in Ireland. Inspired by the success of the French Revolution, many traditional songs were written about the search for freedom for the Irish people (Hast & Scott, 2004). Also during this time of renewal, many people were contributing to the preservation of Irish culture and language. Two of the earliest known collectors, named William and John Neale, were members of the Protestant elite in Ireland. Together father and son compiled the first real collection of exclusively Irish folk music. *A Collection of the Most Celebrated Irish Tunes Proper for Violin, German Flute or Hautboy* was published in Dublin in 1726, and it contained tunes attributed to the last great Irish harper, Turlough Carolan, and others that are still performed today (O Canainn, 1993).

One of the greatest contributors to the preservation of the old Irish harp tradition was Edward Bunting. In the late eighteenth century, four festivals were organized to revitalize the harp tradition. In 1792 Bunting, a Belfast organist, was hired to notate the music performed by ten of Ireland's greatest living harpists at the Belfast Harp Festival. By accepting this position, he became the first Irish collector to obtain music directly from musicians in the field (Sawyers, 2000). After the festival ended, Bunting followed the harpists home to take down more music and learn about their technique. It was the last time that any number of the great harpists would play together and the only time that their music would be written down (O Canainn, 1993). Unfortunately, when Bunting published his three volumes of music, including *General Collection of the Ancient Music of Ireland*, he added elaborate piano arrangements that reflected his classical training and not in the style of the music he had transcribed. Nevertheless, his work was extremely impressive for the time and is still a primary source on the old style of harp playing (Fleischmann, 1952).

At the beginning of the nineteenth century, references to music making in rural Ireland are plentiful. Music dating from this period reflects the changes that were occurring in Irish society. As the English and Protestant elite evicted small farmers from their land, the displaced began to look to other countries in search of a better life. Between 1815 and 1844 over one million Irish immigrated to North America. Songs like "The Green Fields of Canada" reflected the sobering reality that many of these men and women would never see their families or Ireland again. At the same time, those across the Atlantic and in Ireland were composing a form of song most popularly known as "come all ye" ballads. Meant to give a warning or moral lesson to the listener, many of these songs, like "Edward Connors," warned emigrants that America was not as glorious as others might make it seem (Hast & Scott, 2004).

While traditional singing was flourishing in the rural areas of Ireland despite these hardships, the poet Thomas Moore was transforming Irish song into popular parlor music for the middle- and upper-class audiences on both sides of the Atlantic. Between 1808 and 1832 he published ten volumes of songs entitled *Irish Melodies*. Combining author-composed English lyrics and melodies based on old airs, many of which were taken from the Bunting collection, Moore created songs that celebrated the glories of an ancient Celtic Ireland (Hast & Scott, 2004). Although Moore's ballads were far removed from the traditional style of singing in Irish, his work provided a means for many Irish people to reconnect with the music and idealized history of their own country (Fleischmann, 1952).

The reality of Ireland in the 1800s was that 80 percent of the people were Catholic and Irish speakers, and the majority of them were living in dire poverty. The poor inhabited small rural communities called *clachans* that were run by Anglo-Protestant and English landlords and government officials. Those Catholics who could afford to rent large farms divided their property into smaller plots and leased them to people called "cotters." These people occupied a small cottage on the plot in return for services. Rent was high on these plots, and there was no security of tenure. If a family fell destitute, there was no welfare system to assist them, and so many were forced to move to the workhouses in the city. Both in the city and the country the living situation was dreadful and unsafe. Food was scarce, and the poor depended on potatoes for the majority of their nutrition. It was this class of people that the infamous potato famine of 1845–1849 affected the most (Sawyers, 2000).

By the time the Great Famine, or *an Gorta Mór*, ended, 1.5 million people had died of starvation and disease, and 1.6 million more had emigrated. The famine and the years that followed brought with them a time of complete musical silence. Memories of death, illness, evictions, of cottages being burned to the ground by the landlord's henchmen, of the loss of the majority of Irish speakers to emigration, were too horrible and too vivid to put down in words. It wasn't until several years later that even a piece of music was composed about the dark years (Sawyers, 2000).

After the famine ended, a push for home rule or self-government began. Supporters of this movement used Irish language and the glories of the Gaelic past to promote their nationalist agenda. In 1893 the Gaelic League formed, with the primary purpose of promoting Irish values through a revival of the Irish language. Traditional music was used to "sweeten the pill" of language learning and to bring people together into a community (Hast & Scott, 2004). In an effort to reach this goal, the league founded the Musical Festival Association in 1895 and hosted the first Feis Ceoil (pronounced "fesh kee-ool"), or a musical festival involving competitions, in Dublin in 1897 (Pine, 1998). By the closing of the weeklong feis, thirty-two competitions had occurred, with awards given in each category (Vallely, 1999).

As the Gaelic League strove to renew pride and ownership of the music and dance of Ireland, across the country many men and women were fighting for the freedom to rule themselves. On Easter Monday in 1916 one thousand Irish captured strategic buildings in Dublin and proclaimed Irish independence. Eighteen thousand British troops were brought in to regain control of the city. During the aftermath of the Easter Rising, the British executed many of the home rule leaders, and their martyrdom fueled the fight for independence. In 1922 home rule was achieved with the founding of the Irish Free State. The British granted twenty-six of the thirty-two counties independence, if they agreed to still claim allegiance to the British Crown. The remaining six counties, which had a distinct Protestant and pro-British majority, remained directly under British rule. In 1948 the Republic of Ireland became a fully independent country, while to this day Northern Ireland remains a member of the United Kingdom (Hast & Scott, 2004).

THE DAWN OF THE FREE IRISH REPUBLIC

Shortly after the establishment of the Irish Free State, Radio Éireann, Ireland's first radio service, was created. Beginning in 1926, Radio Éireann broadcast programs from their studios in Dublin that included the performance of Irish traditional music. In 1947 the national radio station expanded its capabilities to include a mobile recording unit, which allowed performers from all parts of the country to be broadcast from the station in Dublin without any traveling on the part of the musicians. For the first time, regional styles from places such as Arranmore Island and Valencia, County Kerry, could be heard and learned from throughout Ireland (Vallely, 1999). During the 1920s and 1930s, North American recording companies were promoting Irish traditional dance music. Recordings of musicians such as Michael Coleman, Paddy Killoran, and James Morrison that were made in the United States returned to Ireland and introduced new repertoire and playing styles to rural musicians all over the country. These recordings still are considered valuable today and are continuing to influence the style and technique of current traditional musicians on both sides of the Atlantic (Hast & Scott, 2004).

CEILI BANDS

Prior to the mid 1930s the main venues for social dancing in Ireland were the houses and crossroads. House dances often served as fund-raisers for neighbors or a cause in need of money. They could be held at anyone's house and often were hosted by people not favored by the church or law. During the beginning of the 1930s, the Catholic Church embarked on a state-backed campaign to rid the countryside of these wayward dancers and musicians. In 1935 the state created the Public Dance Hall Act, which permanently changed the Irish dance tradition (Sawyers, 2000). The Dance Hall Act stipulated that all dances must be licensed and operated under strict supervision (Curtis, 1994). This act basically rendered set dancing obsolete and for the first time forced social dancing to shift from the private space to the clergy-organized commercial and morally correct venue (Vallely, 1999).

In an effort to adjust to the larger and new performing venue, traditional musicians formed ceili ("kay-lee") bands consisting of standard traditional instruments as well as drums, piano, saxophone, and double bass. These instruments were added to augment the sound of the music and allow it to be heard in the larger dance hall. Two of the most famous bands of this genre were the Kilfenora Ceili Band and Tula Ceili Band, both originating from County Clare, Ireland (Curtis, 1994). As the ceili moved from the fireside to the commercial dance hall, smaller informal ensemble playing also began to shift to the public venue. Traditional musicians began to gather in pubs to share tunes and perform for anyone who was present at the time. This use of the pub as a venue for informal and social music making has continued in Ireland and the Irish diaspora through the present time (Hast & Scott, 2004).

COMHALTAS CEOLTÓIRÍ ÉIREANN

In 1952 the Comhaltas Ceoltóirí Éireann ("kol-tus kyol-tori air-in"), or CCÉ, was established with the goal to promote Irish traditional music and dance and the Irish language. Today the CCÉ is still based out of Dublin and has over four hundred branches in Ireland, as well as ten more in other countries. Since its conception, the organization has targeted young people as the key to keeping traditional music in circulation. The founders of the Comhaltas created and administered a tiered system of competition called the Fleadh Cheoil ("kee-ohl") in music, singing, and dancing at the county, regional, provincial, and all-Ireland levels. Competition was divided into four age levels: under twelve, twelve to fifteen, fifteen to eighteen, and the senior or over-eighteen classes. Within those age levels a solo competition takes place for every major instrument, including whistling and lilting, and there are group competitions in instrumental playing, ceili bands, and set dancing.

From the beginning of the *fleadhanna* (regional music festival) tradition, winning an All-Ireland title was the highest achievement for many young musicians, and these types of competitions have been a major force in the sponsorship of traditional Irish music during the last fifty years (Hast & Scott, 2004). In the Irish diaspora, *feiseanna* (arts and culture festival that includes Irish step dancing competitions) have motivated children to learn, perform, and excel in traditional Irish music and dance, as well as provided a venue for emigrant families to gather, socialize, and share their music when it might not otherwise be possible. Since the 1970s events such as these have also been used as visible symbols of identity in expanding multicultural societies outside of Ireland (Hast & Scott, 2004).

While the Comhaltas Ceoltóirí Éireann was trying to guarantee the continuation of Irish traditional music in the 1950s and 1960s through the organization of fleadh cheoils throughout Ireland, the composer Seán Ó Riada was gathering traditional musicians together to perform in a different manner. In reaction to the unison performance of the ceili band, Ó Riada developed an approach that allowed the traditional musicians to play passages with various other members present in the ensemble. Also, he provided instrumentalists with opportunities to harmonize with each other within the context of the piece. Out of these experimentations Ó Riada created Ceoltóirí Chualann, and this group featured performers like Paddy Moloney, who would later go on to form The Chieftains. Through the formal stage performances of Ceoltóirí Chualann, the radio programs he hosted, and the music scores for film he composed, Ó Riada reintroduced the general public to how exciting and interesting Irish traditional music could be and instilled in the people at the time a renewed sense of pride in the Irish culture (Vallely, 1999).

THE AMERICAN FOLK REVIVAL AND ITS EFFECT ON IRISH MUSIC

In the early 1960s the folk revival in the United States began to have a great effect on Irish traditional music. The ballad singing revival that produced groups like the Weavers and Peter, Paul, and Mary also turned Irish American singers like the Clancy Brothers and Tommy Makem into overnight successes. The Clancy Brothers' performances of traditional ballads and folk songs in New York City resulted in a revival of the tradition at home in Ireland. This renewal of folk singing can be seen in the formation of singing groups like the Dubliners and the Furey Brothers in the late sixties (Curtis, 1994). At the same time Seán Ó Riada's Ceoltóirí Chualann ceased to perform as an ensemble and Paddy Moloney was beginning to form The Chieftains, a group that would influence Irish traditional music for generations to come. Using and expanding upon many of the same musical concepts that Ó Riada valued, The Chieftains have become "the most traveled and best known group playing Irish traditional music in its purest form" (Curtis, 1994, p. 22).

During the 1970s, Irish traditional music began to interact with both the most ancient roots of the tradition as well as musical traditions from America and Europe. The formation of the Irish folk music band Planxty created an environment for the re-creation of pure traditional tunes and songs in a new manner. Respectful of the roots of Irish music, members of the band Planxty and other similar bands returned to play and trade tunes at informal sessions with other musicians in and around Dublin. The time spent learning tunes in local pubs had a direct influence on the music material Planxty chose to record and perform in concert. The work of groups like The Chieftains and Planxty in the traditional realm ushered in a new era of Irish music that included the innovative group the Bothy Band (Curtis, 1994). Among its many contributions to the tradition, the Bothy Band opened up traditional Irish music to a much younger audience. Professor Mícheál Ó Súilleabháin, director of the University of Limerick Irish World Academy of Music and Dance, believes that the younger audience's involvement in this musical style "is the single greatest factor in the present international interest in Irish traditional music" (Curtis, 1994, p. 26).

Unfortunately, the Bothy Band separated prior to the end of the 1970s, and it was left to groups like Clannad and De Danann to carry the music into the next decade. Clannad's experimentation with the mystical sounds of Irish music helped to lead the youngest member, Enya, into a successful solo career in the years to follow. When studying the traditional music scene of the 1980s, one can divide it into two distinct groups: the professional, commercial musicians, and the amateur musician who played for the love of the music. The latter group of traditional instrumentalists and singers could be found in pubs and singing clubs throughout the country. In the professional realm, solo performers like Sharon Shannon, Mary Black, and Christy Moore were replacing the large groups from previous decades as the new representatives of Irish culture throughout the world.

THE 1990s TO THE PRESENT

The dawn of the 1990s saw the tide turn once again and the formation of new traditional groups in Ireland, like Altan and Dervish, and, in the United States, Cherish the Ladies (Curtis, 1994). Partially fueled by Bill Whelan's *Riverdance*, interest in Irish music once again spread throughout the world. Opening on April 30, 1994, *Riverdance*, which began as a seven-minute interlude during the Eurovision Song Contest, introduced a whole new audience to a noncompetitive, more relaxed, and more experimental version of Irish step dancing and traditional music (Sawyers, 2000). Over a decade later, *Riverdance* and the many other companies that have developed on the coattails of its original success are still performing around the globe, providing professional performance opportunities for traditional musicians and dancers that hadn't been available prior to the 1990s.

While *Riverdance* was touring the globe, people in the academic realm in Ireland were striving to ensure a place for the study, performance, and preservation of Irish music within their own borders. In 1991 the Irish Traditional Music Archive opened in Dublin, and to this day it provides an invaluable resource for historic and contemporary Irish culture. The archive houses manuscripts of collectors such as Bunting, Petrie, and Breathnach and with the assistance of the staff can be accessed and studied by the public (Curtis, 1994). At the collegiate level, Mícheál Ó Súilleabháin founded the Irish World Music Centre at the University of Limerick in 1994. It began as a graduate program designed to incorporate the study of Irish traditional music with other world music traditions. This graduate-level education perfectly complemented the undergraduate study that was occurring at University College Cork and other similar institutions at the time (Hast & Scott, 2004). Now known as the Irish World Academy for Music and Dance, it offers bachelor's, master's, and doctorate programs in a variety of areas.

Also in the 1990s, Ireland embarked on a plan to promote Irish as the national language by requiring its instruction in the national schools. Specifically, at the primary level the 1999 curriculum revision outlined that "arts education is integral to the primary education in helping to promote thinking, imagination and sensitivity, and arts activities can be a focus for social and cultural development and enjoyment in schools" (Gilmore, 1999, p. 2). In the 1999 music curriculum, the learning of the tin whistle, songs in Irish, and tune types are included as required parts of every primary school child's education.

Today the work of traditional musicians from across Ireland and beyond has resulted in the formation of summer music schools like the Willie Clancy Summer School, which has been educating the young and old in one-week sessions in Miltown Malbay since 1973. Recognized as Ireland's foremost venue for teaching traditional music, the Willie Clancy Summer School was created to commemorate the life of one of the leading traditional musicians of the twentieth century through the continuation of the transmission of Irish traditional music. Over thirty years after its establishment, the school is still setting standards for the study and practice of traditional music (Kearns & Taylor, 2003). Also, festivals hosted during the year throughout Ireland provide visitors and natives alike with the opportunity to listen and perform with many of the great musicians currently performing within the tradition.

Although these developments are critical to the continuation of the tradition, it is the traditional music sessions that occur in pubs throughout Ireland seven days a week that remind us all of the roots and history behind the Irish heritage and culture. Visitors to these sessions should be aware of the proper etiquette of these gatherings, including the role of the session leader, the appropriate time for singing and dancing, and the role of socializing that occurs between the tunes. J. Gleeson, in his interview with Dorothea E. Hast, remarked, "It is customary for people to talk while listening to instrumentalist play in a session, but if someone is singing, then that's the one time, the only thing I want to hear is the big clock ticking. And you know when you can hear the clock ticking that you have silence" (Hast & Scott, 2004, p. 4). Through the songs and the tunes and the stories told between the music, the Irish culture is passed on to future generations, ensuring its ultimate survival.

One cannot possibly expect to highlight all that Irish music has to offer in the span of one chapter. Accordingly, this overview should be used as an entry point into the world of Irish traditional music and a guide to outline the many changes and hardships the Irish and their culture have weathered. In the 2000 United States Census, 30,524,799 people marked their ethnic origin as Irish. Many of those listed are children currently going through the American education system. To not address Irish music in the elementary and secondary school world music surveys would be a great disservice not only to those students who are of this heritage but to those who do not realize the influence that the Irish tradition had and still has on our own American folk tradition. It is through the study of Irish music in its historical context that we will be able to understand the role Irish music played in the development of a traditional culture both within its own borders as well as our own.

3

Teaching at Home: The Transmission of Irish Traditional Music and Dance by Irish Teachers in Formal and Informal Settings

Learning traditional music and dances in the classroom, outside their natural informal setting, affects the structuring of a student's habitus and identity. A person's habitus can be defined as a set of dispositions that develop as a result of living in a particular culture. These dispositions generate particular practices and perceptions that are unique and indicative to the culture the student lives in. Most traditions were historically rural based and constructed around certain customs that accompany such lifestyles. The habitus of performers living and learning in that environment are encoded from the past and brought into the present, where they are learned. This learning predisposes the singer or instrumentalist to certain musical habits in the future. When the context for education shifts, it is easy to assume that those who learn in this new environment will have a slightly different view of themselves in regard to the tradition from those who were taught by a master teacher within the traditional community. Across the water from Ireland in the United States, the structuring of the lessons within a unit on Irish music and dance, taught by an American teacher, directly affects what students know and recognize as belonging to the tradition. Even within Ireland the knowledge of the tradition is affected by the construction of learning experiences within the classroom. In each of these circumstances, the traditional values inscribed in the music and dances find their way into the classroom, even when many of the old approaches to studying the genres are lost.

When I first commenced the field research for my book, my plan was to observe several primary school teachers engaging their students in Irish traditional music and dance within the classroom. I chose to study only teachers working in large, formal classroom settings, keeping in mind the transference of techniques to the typical American music-learning environment. It was my intention to discern the materials and methods used in formal settings to teach

Irish music. This proved to be more difficult than I thought it would be. In Ireland, teachers in primary schools (equivalent to United States elementary schools) are expected to teach all subjects, including physical education, art, and music. Every area has its own national curriculum that must be followed, and the music curriculum includes instruction in traditional and classical styles. The minimal third-level training (United States college or university) for Irish primary school teachers in music and dance frequently results in a situation where the majority of music instruction is largely associated with one or two of the faculty members in the school. Dance instruction is routinely separated far away from its natural counterpart, music, and situated within the physical education curriculum.

Upon this discovery I was faced with a decision. As a music teacher, I use dance frequently within my curriculum, although it is not the key concept I am trained to teach. Nevertheless, due to the fact that a vast majority of the traditional Irish tunes in existence today are classified as dance tunes, dance steps must be recorded and taught to American students in order to complete an overview of the interconnectedness of the two traditions in their natural environment (Hast & Scott, 2004). In this book, the method used to transmit Irish dancing in a structured setting by highly qualified teachers in select national schools, and in the private studio by independent teachers, is highlighted as more representative of the tradition than what is represented in the Irish Primary School Physical Education Curriculum. Educators in both these settings have been trained in Irish traditional music and dance in the traditional manner and use their knowledge as a base for their teaching in more formalized settings. The vast majority of dance students currently studying at third-level institutions, such as the University of Limerick, were trained in formal settings by independent teachers rather than by the primary school faculty. In regard to music, I studied two well-respected Irish traditional musicians, Denis Liddy and Michelle Mulcahy, who are teaching primary school children in large groups within the national schools and in a more informal setting. The information gathered from these observations greatly informed the construction of the Irish cultural unit found in chapter 4. By focusing on three particular teaching situations that were similar to my own, I could observe how three teachers within the tradition transmit their knowledge to primary-school-age children, thereby achieving my original goal.

IRISH TRADITIONAL MUSIC'S ROLE HISTORICALLY IN THE PRIMARY SCHOOL CURRICULUM

Since the inception of formal schools in Ireland, teachers have been faced with the challenge of representing classical and traditional music as equally legitimate parts of Irish heritage and cultural identity. As early as the 1700s, England created schools in Ireland with the intent of teaching the "poor natives" the English tongue and principles of true religion and loyalty. In 1831 the English introduced national schools in hopes of improving the social and cultural life of the Irish. According to Marie McCarthy (1999), in these schools music was used to socialize and civilize the "barbaric" youth. Since the melodies of Thomas Moore were esteemed so highly in upper-middle-class Irish society, Moore's "quasi-Irish parlor music found an honored place in the music curriculum of Irish schools at this time" (McCarthy, 1999, p. 41). Also during the nineteenth century, a similar situation was unfolding in the Catholic private schools, where music was used to promote and reinforce religious doctrine and traditions and inculcate high-society values (McCarthy, 1999). In all of these formal education settings, classical music was addressed, while Irish traditional music was dismissed as primitive and unworthy of being taught.

In the early twentieth century the teaching of music began to be valued by the English and the Catholic Church in the national schools as a medium for establishing self and group discipline, for confronting moral issues, and for linking home, school, and society. During the same century, when the cultural nationalist movement occurred, music became an important expression of national identity. In the early years of independence, the role of traditional music was central to the discussion of Irish cultural development. Transmission of traditional music became institutionalized in informal, more traditional schools that aligned themselves in some respects with the traditions of school music (McCarthy, 1999).

During the 1920s, intensive efforts were made to document and publish Irish song repertoire. Each song was accompanied by tonic *sol–fa* notation (commonly used in the Christian Brothers schools to read music), thus enshrining traditionally unwritten repertoire into a fixed, literate form. A standard version of songs was made available to schools, and these editions set up expectations and standards of performance throughout the country for Irish traditional song in the formal school setting (McCarthy, 1999).

While this practice was put in place, the development of the traditional vocal style within the primary and secondary school classroom was met with many obstacles. First of all, the loss of the Irish language as a vernacular affected the transmission of traditional vocal music. Many teachers were unable to sing in Gaeilge (Irish), and as a result traditional singing occurred on a teacher-per-teacher basis, in many cases surviving only in the regions where singing still flourished in the community (Mac Aoidh, 1996). Also, the transmission of Irish music in the colonial nation had not been organized formally in schools. As a result, no infrastructure was in place to support its transmission when socioeconomic and demographic conditions shifted in the middle decades of the twentieth century. This problem, combined with the lack of a clear definition of what traditional Irish music was and the direction it was going, impeded the transmission of the music in the formal music institutions throughout Ireland.

This confusion resulted in a variety of solutions on how to teach music, particularly at the primary school level, where music specialists were not frequently present. From the 1930s until the 1960s, school bands became a popular way to experience music in schools. Consisting of whistle, harmonica, accordion, and percussion, the groups bridged the gap between school and community. Frequently these bands would perform and be judged at musical festivals held outside the school day. Similar to the *feiseanna* run by the Comhaltas, these festivals quickly became the nucleus around which much school music developed. Once again these groups existed in areas where traditional performers were present to transmit the traditional music culture to the students in schools. It wasn't until the 1980s that music would even be mentioned as a necessary component of the primary school curriculum in any educational document produced by the Irish government (McCarthy, 1999).

In 1999 the Irish government produced a new music curriculum for the primary schools. After reviewing the primary school music curriculum, I found that the only major structural difference between the Irish and American music standards is the person responsible for the transmission of music to children of that age. In the vast majority of the American states, music specialists are responsible for the instruction of music. In Ireland it is the duty of the general classroom teacher to teach the music program based on its "close link with other arts subjects and integration with other areas of the curriculum" (Primary School Music Curriculum, 1999, p. 8).

Divided into infant, first and second class, third and fourth class, and fifth and sixth class, the primary school music curriculum is based on the philosophy of sound before symbol. It is assumed that within each grade level, students will move from the known to the unknown, from the simple to the complex, and from experience to a conscious understanding of that experience. During third and fourth classes the curriculum, as in all levels, is divided into three learning strands: listening and responding, performing, and composing. These strands offer teachers a sequenced, comprehensive program on which to base the teaching and learning of music. While the authors of the curriculum encourage primary school teachers to introduce the songs and dances of world cultures within a common musical experience, this learning approach is not applied to their native music and dance. Instead the National School Teacher Guidelines state that on leaving primary school, children should have developed an awareness and appreciation of traditional Irish instruments—tin whistle, Irish flute, uilleann pipes, bodhran, fiddle, concertina, accordion as well as Irish harp—and should have listened to a variety of Irish music (dance, ballad, suantrai [lullaby], work songs, etc.) and musicians. (Arts Education Teacher Guidelines, 1999, p. 57)

This directly reflects the separation of music and dance between the arts and physical education curricula.

IRISH TRADITIONAL MUSIC IN PRACTICE IN THE PRIMARY SCHOOLS

Today access to music education in general is determined by the presence of music specialists in schools and availability of media and technology. Although traditional instrumental and vocal music has a recognized position in the curriculum, the focus has been placed on teaching children how to sing traditional songs in English rather than play an instrument. If instrumental music is taught in a primary classroom, students are more likely to "learn airs on a recorder than dance tunes on a tin whistle" (O'Flynn interview, see appendix). This is a result of the lack of training at third-level teaching institutions in Irish traditional music and the lack of tutors and materials to aid in the teaching of traditional instruments in the primary school classroom by educators outside the tradition.

One may wonder why this might happen in a country that has such a rich history of traditional music. First of all, the aurality of the tradition requires each teacher to have his or her knowledge of tunes and songs to pass on to the students. Frequently, if a person did not grow up with traditional Irish instrumental or vocal music in his or her home, these resources would be difficult to gather. Furthermore, the pedagogical orientation used in the teaching of traditional music (one-on-one lessons, use of rote learning techniques, solo nature of performance, and lack of standard notation) vastly differs from the methods normally used within the formal classroom. Finally, music is only one of the many subjects that preservice primary school teachers have to study during their four years at university.

Located in Limerick, Ireland, Mary Immaculate College prepares 40 percent of the primary school teachers in the country. According to Dr. John O'Flynn (interview, see appendix), a current professor at St. Patrick's College in Dublin and former professor of music education for nine years at Mary Immaculate College, the "average primary school teacher would have about forty hours of music over the whole degree." In that time prospective teachers would be expected to cover the key areas of composing, listening, and performing. Most of the performing would consist of singing, and the music education lecturers at Mary Immaculate College provide their students with a song resource book that contains representative samples of repertoire they feel are "good to use in classroom practice" (O'Flynn interview, see appendix). O'Flynn also acknowledged that the music department does not "have the ability to teach people instruments in groups due to the lack of resources to meet the needs of the four hundred preservice teachers" (interview, see appendix). During our meeting in November 2005, O'Flynn highlighted that the study of traditional instruments of the world would constitute a quarter of the students' listening requirements. He also acknowledged that the lack of training specifically in the Irish instrumental tradition prior to entering the classroom was worrisome.

The creators of *The Music Box*, the standard music textbook used within the third and fourth class, try to compensate for a teacher's lack of knowledge of traditional Irish music by including four songs from the tradition in each level. Two of these songs are solely in Irish, and two are macaronic—that is, in Irish and English. Teachers are encouraged to have the students listen to each piece and learn the chorus of it. Unfortunately, within the suggested lesson the context of the song is only briefly discussed, and it is assumed that the students will be able to translate and understand the long Irish verses by listening independently. Musicians within the tradition acknowledge this lack of Irish representation and have created resources specifically for children. Since the early 1990s Pádraigín Ní Uallacháin, Len Graham, and Garry Ó Briain have researched, collected, and recorded children's songs belonging to the Irish tradition. Complete with translations, and explanations of the song's origin and the story line, the CDs are excellent resources for those less familiar with the repertoire. Additional materials such as *Moon Penny* by Bill Meek, and *So Early in the Morning*, a collaborative work between the Clancy family of Carrick-on-Suir, County Tipperary, Diane Hamilton, and Seamus Ennis, also provide teachers with a wealth of songs that are accessible and appropriate for children.

While the third and fourth class music curriculum states that students should be able to identify and perform simple tunes (such as Irish jigs) from memory or from notation, *The Music Box 3 and 4* do not contain any lessons constructed to this end. The first attempt by traditional musicians to create such a resource for primary school teachers was completed by Brian and Eithne Vallely in the 1970s. In their *Sing a Song and Play It* books, they strove to introduce traditional music into the national schools in Northern Ireland through a three-year course on Irish music and song (McCarthy, 1999). More recently the Web-based company MadForTrad (www.madfortrad.com)

has created a CD-ROM program with the aim of teaching students how to play the instruments used in Irish traditional music.

When traditional instrumental music is taught in the classroom, it generally occurs in the form of tin whistle instruction. From my interviews with John O'Flynn I was able to surmise that there are two types of teachers introducing the tin whistle. The first category of educators would be people who are general music graduates who can teach the children very well but who are not necessarily traditional musicians. From his experience, O'Flynn stated that this type of person would be "very much linked to the school band where they are playing Irish tunes but not necessarily in a traditional style. They would have whistles, piano, accordion, and drums, that kind of basic school band at the primary school." The second category of educators exist less commonly and would be "teachers in the schools who themselves are quite advanced traditional musicians, and they are teaching in a much more community type of style. In that situation they might have a lot of support for music in the primary school system, and they would have small class meetings, and the teacher would encourage children to play different instruments, and they would all learn the tunes" (O'Flynn interview, see appendix).

TRADITIONAL MUSIC AT BAREFIELD NATIONAL SCHOOL

At Barefield National School in County Clare, Denis Liddy is the one traditional musician on staff. He was born and raised in the county, and his fiddle playing is representative of the regional style. An accomplished musician, he has recorded several CDs and can be seen performing frequently throughout Ireland and the United States. Biweekly he teaches groups of Barefield students how to play Irish traditional music in a large ensemble setting. When I met him in the spring of 2006, the Under 12 Barefield Ceili Band had twenty-two members, some as young as nine years old. They play a variety of instruments, including Irish flute, fiddle, box (button accordion), concertina, and harp and are at various levels of competency. On Tuesday and Thursday afternoons they meet for a half hour to rehearse and learn tunes. The material I collected from my observation of one of these classes was very useful to my research, since the number of students present at the rehearsal and length of meeting time is very similar to most American music classroom situations.

In September, Liddy teaches the ensemble a variety of tunes by rote. He begins by playing a small section of the melody unornamented on the fiddle or singing the note names, and the students repeat it back on their instrument. This process is repeated until the entire tune is learned. Once the students have learned the tune, the ornamentations are added to create the regional flavor. Students are also given CD recordings of the tunes to practice with at home, to reinforce the classroom learning. In addition to learning the repertoire, Liddy spends a great deal of time on ear training with this young group of musicians, to strengthen their aural skills. By the time I observed the Under 12 Barefield Ceili Band in March, their ears had become so well trained that the exercises were no longer needed. Instead, they were able to review the tune once and then spend the rest of the time arranging it.

During the half hour I spent at Barefield National School, Liddy arranged two tunes for the band. The tunes were in binary form, and each section was played twice, to create an AABB structure. Using a similar approach for both pieces, he began by assigning the main tune to one or two instruments, while the others accompanied with chords and drones. On both the melodic and accompanying line older, stronger players were used to support the younger, less-experienced children. However, before deciding on the exact arrangement of the hornpipe they were working on, Liddy had a variety of instruments play the tune and the drones together. Within the ceili band rehearsal, the transmission of the arrangement is carried out in a completely aural method and is frequently reviewed so that the students do not get confused. Due to the tremendous amount of ear training and practice on the part of the students, they are quick to pick up the tune and make any of the necessary adjustments.

The method used by Denis Liddy to pass on traditional Irish tunes to a large group of students in the national schools is almost identical to the process used in the informal learning setting. The emphasis of learning through listening and performing is present in both environments, and it is only the approach to arranging the tunes that differs. In a smaller, less formal situation, musicians would work together to arrange a piece, whereas in the classroom situation the teacher, Liddy, makes all the decisions. The ethnograpic study of Mr. Liddy and students as well as several other traditional teachers' studios has helped me understand how each lesson is situated in a large curriculum and system of music instruction.

IRISH TRADITIONAL MUSIC IN GROUP
LESSONS OUTSIDE THE NATIONAL SCHOOLS

Michelle Mulcahy began learning how to play the tin whistle when she was five years old. Her father, Mick, a well-respected musician in the Irish tradition, was her first teacher. Michelle learned how to play the button accordion by listening to him play and watching him maneuver around the keys. She would later join the local Comhaltas branch, and her tuition (education) in the many instruments she now plays would continue from there. Today Michelle Mulcahy is a tutor to the young and old alike. Whether it is at home in Abbeyfeale, at the local Comhaltas branch, or at festivals such as the Willy Clancy Festival, her teaching style is directly related to the methods of transmission she learned from as a child.

During our interview I asked Mulcahy whether her teaching approach varied depending on the number of students. She was quick to point out that how she teaches depends entirely upon the particular student:

> I adapt to each student's ability and style of learning, so I don't have a set way in teaching every student. However, generally beginners are taught the basics, from scales to fingering positions and so on to intermediate and advanced, where ornamentation and variation is worked upon. Also I give the students a tune to learn by ear, which will help them to develop their aural training. (Mulcahy interview, May 2006)

She said that, "Within larger classes one's teaching style has to change slightly" (Mulcahy interview, May 2006). She continued by describing the process she follows in this type of situation. First she would begin by recording the tune on tape for all the students, at a slow and then medium pace. Then she would write out the basic tune. She feels this helps both the students who want to learn by ear and those who learn by notes. Although she provides written notation to her pupils, she continually emphasizes the need to listen to the recording of the tune in order to grasp how the basic tune is ornamented. Although the development of students' aural skills will assist in their "picking up" of ornamentation and variation, which is then incorporated into their individual style, Mulcahy stresses the importance of allowing students to develop their own interpretation of the tune without any outside influences.

In the cases of both Mulcahy, located in the larger Irish traditional education community, and Liddy, within the national school system, their backgrounds as musicians inform their method of transmission. Although their situations are slightly different, the process of "passing on" the tune is identical. First, the basic tune is played slowly by the teacher and repeated by the student. Then the tempo is gradually increased as the children's ears become accustomed to leading the learning. Eventually, after much listening, ornamentation is added to give each individual his or her own unique style. While this proves the point that traditional music can be taught in the formal school setting in an accurate manner, I still felt that teachers outside the tradition might need a little more direction in the approach to "passing on" the Irish culture. Consequently I asked Mulcahy what advice she would give someone who had not grown up in a similar musical environment in regard to the preparation and execution of a fiddle lesson in a formal setting. She said,

> I would recommend recordings for the teacher to go and listen to music first. This listening should be focused around the music of different musicians who are considered to be of seminal importance within the tradition. From that they would be able to hear the style of fiddle playing that appeals to them, a style that would influence them in their musical learning. This listening selection would then be given to the student. When teaching a beginner fiddle player I would start with the basic fiddle technique. Then I would explain the different tune types within the tradition and play them an example. After that I [the teacher] would advise them [the student] to keep listening to recordings and maybe start attending the workshops at different music festivals. This would give them an opportunity to hear and learn from other fiddle players within the tradition, which would encourage them to develop an individual style of playing. (Mulcahy interview, May 2006)

This type of information, in combination with ethnographies of lessons (studies that aim to describe the nature and process used by the people being studied) taught by Irish musicians and educators, would be of great use to pre-service primary school teachers. It would provide them with an understanding of how people within the tradition construct the transmission of music in large group settings. The structures established for the transmission of Irish traditional music in the formal music setting will greatly shape all facets of the future of music for the entire country. If there is not an increase in the transmission of the dance music and songs of Ireland within the primary school classroom in the near future, the repertoire this generation will know to pass on to the next will be limited. Without repertoire, there will not be any innovation or change in the tradition in future years. This will result in a loss of depth and richness in the tradition. Preservice teachers need more extensive training at the university level in the methods of transmission of Irish music. This preparation should include techniques used by traditional musicians in informal and formal contexts. The additional time spent on this particular area of Irish culture would help to prepare graduates to teach all of the children of Ireland about the music of their country (Mac Aoidh, 1996).

TRADITIONAL DANCING IN THE NATIONAL SCHOOLS

The role dance plays in the primary schools is very similar to that of music. As part of the relatively new physical education curriculum, dance is required to be included in the physical activities the classroom teacher creates for the students. Although the curriculum was established in 1999, the in-service for teachers on how to approach integrating dance into their already established practice did not occur until the 2005–2006 school year. While some educators do provide students with dance experience, the majority of educators do not. Upon taking an informal survey of the students studying for their bachelor of arts in traditional music and dance at the Irish World Academy of Music and Dance, I discovered that most of the students had been taught Irish set dances at school by a teacher from outside the normal faculty. Usually a trained dancer within the tradition, this person would visit the school weekly to instruct the students on traditional set, ceili, and step dancing in much the same manner that the dance masters did historically in rural Ireland. In Cahirciveen and at the national schools in the surrounding area such as Valentia Island, Waterville, and Ballinskelligs, Ms. Ina Fitzpatrick is that person.

Ina Fitzpatrick was born and raised in Cahirciveen, County Kerry, and began dancing as a small child. In 2000 she started a dance studio. During the week she travels to the national schools in the area and teaches set dances to all the students. Several nights a week and on Saturday morning she also teaches classes at her private studio. While her instruction in the schools is primarily focused on the transmission of Irish set and ceili dances, the children who study with her at her studio are introduced to traditional step, set, and other dance forms from outside Ireland. Using poems, well-planned warm-ups and games, Ina teaches her students the rudiments of the traditional dance form. At the start of the beginner level dance class, her students chant the poem she has taught them: "Palms out, hide your thumb and make a fist. Arms at your side, head pulled up by the magic string and two heavy shoulders" (Fitzpatrick ethnography, see appendix). It is clear to any observer that her teaching reflects a thorough understanding of the process of learning that needs to occur for her students to enjoy and be successful in their initial traditional dance experiences.

Dance and the accompanying music are not separated when traditional steps are taught. Instead, the steps, introduced one section at a time, are sung to an appropriate tune so that students will automatically understand the timing of the dance. When I traveled to Cahirciveen to observe Fitzpatrick, the fifteen students present were in the process of learning the second figure of the South Kerry Set. After a great deal of instruction, they had learned it well enough to dance the figure from start to finish. Before attempting their first run-through with the CD recording, Ina partnered older and younger children together to provide them with the most successful experience possible. Also, on the last step of the previous phrase she would call out the next step to prepare the dancers for what was ahead.

The transmission of Irish dancing to beginning dance students in the large group setting is completely aural and identical to the method used in a more traditional one-on-one setting with my dance tutors at the Irish World Academy of Music and Dance. For example, in both settings the teacher made technical corrections using verbal cues as guides, such as "Cross your feet so that your toes are almost touching" and "Use your back leg to anchor the movement." Also, old material is reviewed in both the individual and group lesson, and one-on-one attention is given to areas of difficulty within the dance. Finally, wrong movements are corrected through the pattern of teacher demonstrates, student tries to imitate. Usually these corrections are made at the same tempo as the rest of the piece; however, when this is not possible, steps can be slowed down and taught at an easier tempo.

The similarity between the primary school and third-level dance teacher's approach seems to indicate that these are standard methods of transmission of Irish step dances. I found it interesting that all steps are taught at the performance tempo and slowed down only when difficulty arose. This was very different from the teaching approach I am used to and something I added into the dance lesson plans I created for the Irish unit. Another aspect of this learning experience that will inform the construction of my book lessons is how important it is to consistently use names for steps so that students will be able to successfully complete them later. Due to the lack of visual representation of terms, it is important that the student instantly understand what step the teacher is referring to when a new dance is introduced. When this is not the case, a lot of time will be spent on bridging the information gap. Finally, as was the case with all the music I have been exposed to, I learned from this experience that dancers are aware of the history their art form is grounded in. As an outsider introducing young students to basic Irish dancing, I will always need to remember to pass on the history as well as the steps.

CONCLUSION

From the interviews and ethnographic experiences I have had in the field, I learned a tremendous amount about the transmission method used by educators instructing large groups of beginning students. Whether it was in a formal classroom or the private studio, the aurality and the history of the tradition are preserved by those who grew up as "insiders" themselves. Unfortunately, this idyllic situation is not the case across Ireland, as I naively assumed it would be when I arrived. Lack of third-level training hinders the consistent transmission of Irish traditional music in the primary classroom across the entire country. As a result, the majority of professional traditional musicians today received most of their training outside the classroom.

Although my research has taken on a slightly different shape from what was originally intended, I do not see that as a sign it was unsuccessful. Quite the contrary, through my fieldwork I was able to determine that it is possible to transmit Irish traditional music in the classroom and study those who, on a daily basis, "pass on" the tradition. The information I collected from my observations has significantly influenced the construction of my unit on Irish traditional music for American elementary students, which will be discussed in the next chapter. I now feel that as a result of my research I am able to create a musical experience that will introduce American students to Ireland in a manner that respects and emphasizes the music's traditional rural and individualistic style.

4

Teaching Abroad: Introducing Irish Traditional Music and Dance to American Students

In the 2000 United States Census, 30,524,799 people marked their ethnic origin as Irish. Many of these Americans participate in their tradition by privately studying Irish music and dance and taking part in festivals and competitions throughout the country. Although the Irish are one of the largest ethnic populations in the United States, very limited resources are available to elementary vocal/general music educators who would like to expose all their students to this tradition.

CREATING AN IRISH TRADITIONAL MUSIC AND DANCE UNIT

One of the key elements to a successful world music unit is the quality and authenticity of the music it uses. Consequently, when I began creating an Irish traditional music and dance unit, I collected songs, tunes, and dances from recordings and performances by traditional musicians throughout Ireland. When working with a primarily oral tradition, notation or lack of it will always be an issue. From this project's inception I sought out guidance on the transcription of tunes and dance steps. However, as a trained singer, I felt I was able to accurately represent the songs without aid. This viewpoint changed as I progressed through my field research, and eventually I approached Sandra Joyce, program director for the bachelor of arts in traditional music at the Irish World Academy of Music and Dance. Together we decided that the basic melody of the songs should be transcribed in staff notation. Then the teacher would learn the style of the music by ear from the accompanying CD recording of the piece.

My approach to creating a lesson format was directly related to my training in the field of ethnomusicology. The study of musical transmission has influenced my approach to curriculum writing. Instead of using "lesson procedure" as I would have in the past, I have used "transmission process" for the lessons in this unit. I feel this simple change of terminology has greatly affected my approach to planning this traditional music unit. It certainly influenced me to divide the lesson into introducing, learning, experiencing, and discussing the tradition. These subcategories have helped me partition each lesson into a clear learning process that is directly influenced by the tradition being taught.

The following pages consist of the unit I created as a result of my research. The songs, tunes, and dances were carefully selected from my recordings in the field. Due to a firm understanding of the general number of lessons a unit requires, I was not able to incorporate all the music I collected. Consequently, the appendix contains the additional material that space limitations prevented me from including. The National Standards for Music Education used in the lesson plans came from the book *National Standards for Arts Education* by the Consortium of National Arts Education Associations (Reston, VA: MENC, 1994).

This unit is meant to introduce educators and students alike to the Irish tradition. The additional songs, dances, and tunes can be used to create further units that build off the knowledge collected for this book. In the "trad" music community the time spent sharing tunes and a song with friends is highly valued. It is a way to share Irish history and music as well as lay the foundation for future musicians in the tradition. As a result, this unit of study ends with a ceili (pronounced "kay-lee"), which is a large social gathering that features music and dancing. I feel this would be the best possible way to assess whether the students understand and respect the material they learned. The student's parents would be invited, and the children would perform the songs, dances, and tunes they learned during the unit. The ceili provides parents with the opportunity to observe what their children are working on in class. With any luck it would broaden their horizons as well.

As Patricia Shehan Campbell said in the second edition of *Multicultural Perspectives for Music Education* (Anderson & Campbell, 1996, p. 2), "The ultimate goal for multicultural education is to provide avenues of exploration so that students can gain a better understanding of the world and of their American heritage." It is my hope that this unit will help achieve that goal.

LESSON 1

Objective: Students will be introduced to Irish traditional music

Goals:

- Students will be able to perform the traditional song "My Aunt Jane."
- Students will have an understanding of the basic conflicts and difficulties that have occurred throughout the history of Ireland and their effect on the tradition.
- Students will be able to hold and produce tones on the tin whistle.

Standards:

- U.S. National Standards for Music Education:
  - ○ 1b: Students will sing expressively with appropriate dynamics, phrasing, and interpretation.
  - ○ 6b: Demonstrate perceptual skills by moving, by answering questions about and by describing aural examples of music of various styles representing diverse cultures.
  - ○ 9b: Identify and describe roles of musicians in various music settings and cultures.

Materials:

- Class set of tin whistles
- Tin whistle fingering chart/tin whistle tutorial videos
- CDs
  - ○ Recorded instrumental selection of the teacher's choice to listen to on the way into class, preferably containing the tin whistle
  - ○ Recording of "Milltown Jig"
  - ○ *When I Was Young* by Len Graham, and Garry Ó Briain, Pádraigín Ní Uallacháin (optional)
  - ○ Transcription and accompanying CD (track 1) of "My Aunt Jane"

Transmission process:

1. Introducing the tradition
- As the students enter the classroom, the teacher will have an Irish tune playing on the CD player. When the students are settled into their seats, the teacher will pause the recording and ask them to discuss with their partner what country the music came from. If they need another listening, the teacher will play it again.

- The class will discuss what country they thought the music was from and what made them think this way. They will listen to it one more time to listen for the certain aspects that make the tune Irish (e.g., instruments, tune melody, is it dance music?).
- The students will locate Ireland on a map, and the teacher, using the attached history outline as a guide, will give a brief overview of the general conflicts and difficulties that have occurred in Ireland and affected the music. (Pictures of the country can be found on Irish tourism websites.)
- The teacher will give the students a few minutes to get up and look at the pictures of Ireland that are spread throughout the room before returning to their seats.

2. Learning the tradition
"My Aunt Jane" (singing).

- The teacher will ask the students to listen carefully to the song about his or her aunt. The teacher will tell the students that at the end of the song they will be asked about what they heard.
- The teacher will sing the song "My Aunt Jane."
  - Meaning of the song: A common fixture in nineteenth-century Irish life was the "wee shop." Found throughout the country, this "wee shop" was the precursor to the modern small grocery store. Located in the third room of one of the villagers' cottages, it sold all the supplies the locals needed (Leyden, 1989). While today this might not be common knowledge among Irish children, "black lumps" is still a term used by some to refer to a type of boiled sweet that much of Europe would call hard candy. This song is one of the most popular songs sung by Ulster schoolchildren.
- The class will discuss what they heard and write out the main ideas for each verse on the board.

> (E.g., verse 1: My Aunt Jane she took me in
> She gave me tea out of her wee tin
> Half a bap with sugar on the top
> Three black lumps out of her wee shop.)

- The teacher will explain the different aspects of the song that the students do not understand.
- The students will learn the melody by rote, and the class will sing the song together.

The "Milltown Jig" (tin whistle).

Step-by-step diagrams of the ornamentation can be found in the appendix (Tin Whistle Ornamentation Guide).Video and audio recordings of the "Milltown Jig" and ornamentations can be found on the accompanying CD.

- The students will be given tin whistles and asked to put them in their laps quietly.
- The teacher will explain to the students about the role that the tin whistle plays in Irish traditional music and where such music is performed (e.g., to accompany dances, found in the large dance shows, played in sessions).
- The teacher will show the students how to hold the tin whistle and where to put their fingers. (If the teacher is unfamiliar with tin whistle technique, *Geraldine Cotter's Traditional Irish Tin Whistle Tutor* is an excellent resource.)
- The teacher will show the students the correct embouchure for the tin whistle.
- The teacher will have students practicethe breathing necessary to produce sound on the tin whistle.
- The teacher will again show the students the fingerings, and they will practice individually while the teacher checks each student's fingering position.
- Students will try to play a few notes together as a class. They will be sent home to practice what they learned.
- As the tin whistles are being put away, the class will listen to the recording of "Milltown Jig."

3. Experiencing the tradition
- The students will watch a brief clip from the original *Lord of the Dance*. In this clip the Little Spirit (dressed all in yellow) plays the tin whistle.
- The class will discuss the performance and how it differs from what they have already heard today.

4. Discussing the tradition
- The class will discuss the differences between the performances they have heard today (one in a traditional style, one in a more modern style). They will discuss whether or not both belong in the traditional music genre.

- The class will review the information they learned today, including the history of Ireland.

5. Closing formulae
- Students will sing "My Aunt Jane" as they line up to leave.
- The teacher will tell the students briefly about the ceili that will occur at the end of the entire unit and hand out an information sheet to take home to their parents.

Assessment (continuous and noncontinuous)
- Students will be evaluated within the lesson on their ability to hold and finger the notes on the tin whistle.
- Students will be evaluated on their singing of "My Aunt Jane" with the class.

Teacher reflection

TIN WHISTLE FINGERING CHART

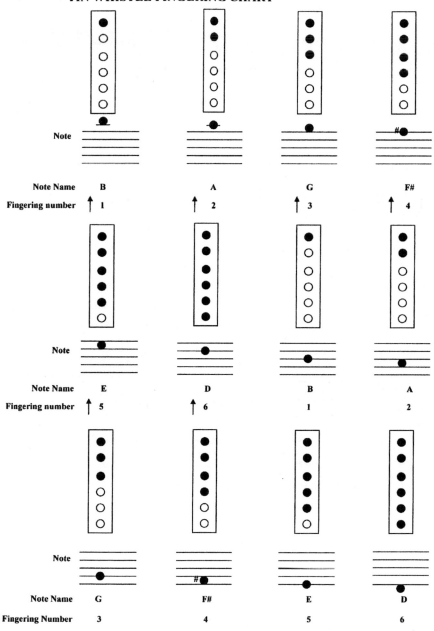

My Aunt Jane

Transcribed by Rebecca Farrell
Learned from "When I Was Young" by
Len Graham, Garry Ó Briain and
Pádraigín Ní Uallacháin

Voice

My aunt Jane she took me in - she gave me tea out of her wee tin

half a bap with sug-ar on the top   three black lumps out of her   wee   shop

Half a bap with sug-ar on the top   three black lumps out of her   wee   shop.

2 My aunt Jane she's awful smart
  she bakes wee rings in an apple tart
  And when Hallow'een comes round
  Forenenst that tart we're always found
  And when Hallow'een comes round
  Forenenst that tart we're always found.

3. My aunt Jane has a bell on the door
   A white stone step and a clean swept floor
   Candy apples, hard green pears
   Conversation lozenges
   Candy apples, hard green pears
   Conversation lozenges

4. My aunt Jane can dance a jig
   And sing a song 'round a sweetie pig
   Wee red eyes and a cord for a tail
   Hanging in a bunch from a crooked nail
   Wee red eyes and a cord for a tail
   Hanging in a bunch from a crooked nail.

5. My aunt Jane she's never cross
   She paid five shillings for an old wooden horse
   She jumped on its back the bones let a crack
   You play the fiddle 'til I get back
   She jumped on its back the bones let a crack
   You play the fiddle 'til I get back.

6. My aunt Jane she took me in
   She gave me tea out of her wee tin
   Half a bap with sugar on the top
   Three black lumps out of her wee   shop
   Half a bap with sugar on the top
   Three black lumps out of her wee , shop

Table 4.1. Outline for History of Irish Music

Time Period	Historical Event	Musical Instrument and Events of Importance
2000 BCE–11th century CE	Early Celts ruled Ireland	Harp was used to accompany the voice.
12th century–16th century	Arrival of the Normans Gaelic chieftains system of patronage	Love songs similar to those of the French and Spanish tradition are integrated into Irish music. Bards and harpists are employed by the Irish aristocracy to compose songs praising and documenting the accomplishments of the patron. When these musicians and poets grew old they would pass their position onto their sons.
17th century	1601—The Battle of Kinsale and the end of the old Gaelic order. The English now ruled Ireland.	Harp was banned from being performed. "Hang the Harpers" decree: traveling harpists were to be hanged wherever they were found.
18th century	Colonialism in Ireland	1792 Belfast Harp Festival, the last time any number of the harpists from the old style would play together and the only time the music was written down. Edward Bunting collected the music from the harp festival and became the first notable collector of Irish music. Publication of Irish traditional songs, dances, and tunes became extremely important (e.g., Petrie and P. W. Joyce's collections preserved much of the music at that time).
19th century	Great Famine (1845–1849) Irish Emigration to America and Australia—American wakes 1893—Gaelic League Push for home rule	Fiddle and pipes used to play dance music, which accompanied the dance masters. "Come All Ye" ballads; broadside ballads. Traditional music is used to help revive the Irish language.
20th century	1916—Easter Rising 1922—Irish Free State founded 1935—Public Dance Hall Act 1951—Comhaltas Ceoltóirí Éireann forms 1950s—Seán Ó Riada puts traditional music on the concert hall stage 1960s—American folk song revival influences Irish traditional song	Harp becomes a sign of the Irish Free State. 1930s—dancing is forbidden to be performed at the crossroads as in the past. Set dancing becomes obsolete. Traditional musicians form ceili bands to perform in the church hall, which is decreed to be the morally correct venue. The most famous bands are the Kilfenora Ceili Band and the Tula Ceili Band. The Clancy Brothers and Tommy Makem—Irish folk song and rebel ballad tradition gains popularity again in Ireland. 1970s—Rise of traditional bands: Planxty, the Bothy Band. 1990s—Irish dance shows like Riverdance.

LESSON 2

Objective: Students will be introduced to step dancing and traditional songs in the Irish language

Goals:

- Students will have an understanding of the historical significance of the song "Óró Sé Do Bheatha 'Bhaile."
- Students will be introduced to the Irish language and be able to sing a chorus of a song in Irish.
- Students will be able to perform one section of a jig step.
- Students will be able to perform the first three bars of the basic "Milltown Jig" tune.

Standards:

- U.S. National Standards for Music Education:
  - 1b: Students will sing expressively with appropriate dynamics, phrasing, and interpretation.
  - 1c: Sing from memory a varied repertoire of songs representing genres and styles from diverse cultures.
  - 2c: Echo short rhythms and melodic patterns.
  - 6b: Demonstrate perceptual skills by moving, by answering questions about, and by describing aural examples of music of various styles representing diverse cultures.
  - 6d: Identify the sounds a variety of instruments, including many orchestra and band instruments and instruments from various cultures, as well as children's voices and male and female voices.
  - 8b: Identify ways in which the principles and subject matter of other disciplines taught in school are interrelated with those of music (history).

Materials:

- Class set of tin whistles
- CDs
  - Recording of "Milltown Jig"
  - *Suantraí: An Irish Lullaby* by Pádraigín Ní Uallacháin (optional)
  - Transcription and accompanying CD (track 2) of "Óró Sé Do Bheatha 'Bhaile"

- DVD or videotape of *Riverdance* (can be found at the local library or purchased on Amazon or Barnes and Noble websites) fast-forwarded to the uilleann pipe solo.

Transmission process:

1. Introducing the tradition
- The teacher will have several Irish words on the board when the students enter the classroom.
  - Examples of possible vocabulary
    - Go raibh maith agat (guh rev mah a-gut) = thank you
    - Sláinte (slawn-tche) = to your health, or "cheers"
    - Éireann go Brách (erin guh brawk) = Ireland forever
    - Dia Duit (jia gwit) = hello
    - Slán Abhaile (slawn awhile-uh) = good-bye
  - The teacher will define what all the words mean.
  - The teacher will say the words, and the students will repeat them after the teacher.
  - The teacher will explain how at one time in Ireland's history everyone spoke Irish. When Ireland became a colony of England, the English queen declared the speaking of Irish to be illegal. The Irish refused to let the Crown prevent them from speaking their native tongue, and so secret "hedge schools" were created throughout the country for the teaching of the language. Today only 4 percent of the Irish population are fluent speakers, even though all students are required to take Irish while enrolled in national schools. Most of these people live in the Gaeltacht or Irish-speaking regions of Ireland. Gaeilge, or the Irish language, is spoken in these regions. In these regions the town names, street signs, and most shop names are written only in Irish. To see pictures of street signs in all Irish go to http://en.wikipedia.org/wiki/Road_signs_in_the_Republic_of_Ireland, or Google "Gaelic street signs."

2. Learning the tradition
- "Óró Sé Do Bheatha 'Bhaile" (Irish-language song).
  - Meaning of the song: Pádraig Pearse wrote this nationalistic song in the early 1900s during the fight for Ireland's freedom. It was meant to call all the Irishmen who were serving in the British army home to fight for their own country and not a foreign empire in a foreign land. Although Pearse wrote the words himself, he did not pen the tune. At the time it was a popular tune in the tradition. The Gráinne Mhaol discussed in the song was a woman pirate from the O'Malley clan of

County Mayo. To learn more about Pearse, a major figure in the Easter Rising of 1916, go to http://en.wikipedia.org and search for either Patrick Pearse or Pádraig Pearse. Additional information on Pádraig Pearse and the Easter Rising can be found in Tim Pat Coogan's book *1916: The Easter Rising.*

○ The teacher will say a few of the words of the *curfá* (chorus), and the students will repeat them. Each time she will add a few words on to what they already know (e.g., first time: óró; second time: óró sé do).

○ The teacher will introduce the melody of the curfá to the students one section at a time. (This should be done aurally. Like the instrumental tradition, the Irish song tradition is passed on aurally.) The students will practice the curfá a few times in succession to help their pronunciation.

○ The teacher will encourage the students to join in on the curfá as the teacher sings the entire song.

○ Students will talk about how they felt as they performed the song.

• Introduction to step dancing.

○ The teacher will explain that there are four different types of traditional Irish dancing: step, sean nós, ceili, and set. In the 1800s dancing was an integral part of most Irish people's lives. People would meet at the crossroads out in the country and dance. They would also meet at neighbors' houses and hold a kitchen party where musicians would play and dancers would accompany them with the battering of their feet. In 1930 the Dance Hall Act changed all that. Dancing was forbidden to occur anywhere outside the controlled dance hall. (See history outline.)

○ Prior to the 1900s dance masters traveled the countryside and taught dance steps to people from the villages they passed through. The best students were taught solo step dances, and frequently competitions would be held between these students to determine who was the best. Today that type of competition occurs at a *feis* (pronounced "fesh"). Dancers from different schools compete against each other, and judges decide who is best.

○ The teacher will introduce the jig as the first dance most step dancers learn. The important things to remember are your legs need to be turned out from the hip, you need to be on your toes, and feet need to be crossed with your toes pointed when you kick your leg. Wendy Garofoli wrote a great book called *Irish Dancing*, which is an excellent introduction to Irish dancing at the third- to fourth-grade reading level. This will be an excellent resource for you and your students.

○ The teacher will teach the first chunk of the first jig step, using the key in this chapter following "Óró Sé Do Bheatha 'Bhaile" and singing the steps as she teaches them. (The key is to pick a jig tune that the students will eventually perform the steps to, and fit the step names to the melody of thc tune. That way the students will already know the tune prior to its formal introduction.)

Step front, step back, hop back 2-3-4
Step front, step back, hop back 2-3-4
Step front, step back, hop back 2-3-4
Up hop back, hop back 2-3-4

○ The teacher will practice this with the students.
○ Students will try to perform the jig step with music.
• The "Milltown Jig" (tin whistle)
  ○ The students will be given tin whistles and asked to put them in their laps quietly. (While they get their tin whistle, the recording of "Milltown Jig" will be played.)
  ○ The teacher will review what was learned last week.
  ○ The teacher will review certain fingering patterns with the students in preparation for learning a tune.
  ○ The teacher will introduce the first measure of the basic tune for the "Milltown Jig." (The teacher will play, and the students will echo. See the appendix for tunes.) The number of measures learned today is dependent on the abilities of the class.
  ○ Students will put away their tin whistles.

3. Experiencing the tradition
• At this point, if possible, an uilleann piper will be brought in to talk briefly with the class and perform. If not, the piper solo in *Riverdance* can be watched to show what this important instrument looks and sounds like. The Comhaltas Ceoltóirí Éireann (CCE) is the Irish Musician Society. Branches of the CCE are located all over the United States. To locate a branch near you, go to www.ccenorthamerica.org.

4. Discussing the tradition
• The teacher will lead the students through a discussion of the similarities and differences between the tin whistle and the uilleann pipes.
• The teacher will discuss the importance of the pipes within the Irish music tradition.
• The class will discuss what they have learned today, making connections with the previous week.

5. Closing formulae
- As the students line up, the teacher will sing or have the students listen to an Irish lullaby. One great example is "Suantraí Sí" from Pádraigín Ní Uallacháin's CD *Suantraí: An Irish Lullaby*. This song was written by Pádraigín's brother for his daughter Niabh.

Assessment (continuous and noncontinuous)

- Students will be assessed on their progress on the tin whistle.
- Students' participation in class will be noted.
- Students will be assessed on their ability to perform the tin whistle tune and jig step in order to prepare for next week's lessons.

Teacher reflection

Irish Language Pronunciation Guide

Accented Vowels

á is pronounced as in the English word "drawl"
é is pronounced as in the English word "say"
í is pronounced as in the English word "see"
ó is pronounced as in the English word "home"
ú is pronounced as in the English word "too"

Key Consonants

"fh" in most cases has no sound, so
  "d'fh-" = "d-"
  "b'fh" = "b-"
"ng" is pronounced as in English word "sang"
"ch" is pronounced as in Scottish word "loch" or German word "ach"
"mh," "bh" can be pronounced either as "w" or "v," as in English words
  "woe" or "vote"
"s" after or before "i" or before "e" is pronounced as in English "shy"
"s" after or before "o," "a," "u" is pronounced as in English "dress"

Common Phrases

Dia Duit = God be with you (Hello)
Dia is Muire Duit = God and Mary to you (Hello in reply)
Conas atá tú? = How are you?
Tá mé go maith = I'm doing well
Codladh sámh = A pleasant sleep
Gurab amhlaidh duit = The same to you (said as a reply to a statement like
"Sleep well")
Nollaig shona duit = Happy Christmas
Sláinte = Cheers!
Go raimh maith agat = Thank you
Slán Leat = Good-bye

Óró Sé Do Bheatha 'Bhaile

Transcribed by Rebecca Farrell
Lyrics by Pádraig Pearse
Traditional Melody

2. A bhuí le rí na bhfeart go bhfeiceam
   Muna mem beo'na dhiaidh ach seachtain
   Gráinne Mhaol agus mill gaiscíoch
   Ag fógairt fáin ar Challaibh

Wee le ree na vairt guh veck-um
Moo-na mem byo na yee ahk shock-tun
Graw-nya wail ahgus meel-ya gesh-keekh
Fo-gurt fawn air ghow-liv.

    Curfa

    Chorus

3. Tá Gráinne Mhaol ag teacht thar sáile
   Oglaigh armtha léi mar gharda
   Gaeil iad féin's ni Gaill ná Spáinnigh
   's cuirfid siad ruaig ar Ghallaibh

Taw graw-nya wail egg tyakht har saw-lya
Og-li arm-ha ley may-ar har-da
Gail-eed fain snee gull naw spawn-yee
Goor-eesh air gur-roo gair ghow-liv.

    Curfa

    Chorus

"Óró, Sé Do Bheatha 'Bhaile"

CURFÁ:
Óró, sé do bheatha 'bhaile! Óró, sé do bheatha 'bhaile!
Óró, you are welcome home! Óró, you are welcome home!

Óró, sé do bheatha 'bhaile! Anois ar theacht an tsamhraidh.
Óró, you are welcome home! Now that the summer is coming.

Sé do bheatha a bhean ba léanmhar
Welcome O woman who was so afflicted,

B'é ár gcreach tú bheith i ngéibhinn
It was our ruin that you were in bondage

Do dhúiche bhreá i seilbh méirleach
Our fine land in the possession of thieves,

Is tú díolta leis na Ghallaibh.
Sold to the foreigners.

CURFÁ:
Óró, sé do bheatha 'bhaile! Óró, sé do bheatha 'bhaile!
Óró, you are welcome home! Óró, you are welcome home!

Óró, sé do bheatha 'bhaile! Anois ar theacht an tsamhraidh.
Oro, you are welcome home! Now that the summer is coming

A bhuí le Rí na bhfeart go bhfeiceam
Please the Great God that we may see,

Muna mbeam beo 'na dhiaidh ach seachtain
Although we may only live a week after it

Gráinne Mhaol agus míle gaiscíoch.
Gráinne Mhaol and a thousand warriors,

Ag fógairt fáin ar Ghallaibh
Dispersing the foreigners.

CURFÁ:
Óró, sé do bheatha 'bhaile! Óró, sé do bheatha 'bhaile!
Óró, you are welcome home! Óró, you are welcome home!
Óró, sé do bheatha 'bhaile! Anois ar theacht an tsamhraidh.
Oro, you are welcome home! Now that the summer is coming

Tá Gráinne Mhaol ag teacht thar sáile
Gráinne Mhaol is coming over the sea

Oglaigh armtha léi mar gharda
Armed warriors along with her as a guard

Gaeil iad féin 's ní Gaill ná Spáinnigh;
They are Irish themselves, not foreigners nor Spaniards,

'S cuirfid siad ruaig ar Ghallaibh.
And they will rout the foreigners.

CURFÁ:
Óró, sé do bheatha 'bhaile! Óró, sé do bheatha 'bhaile!
Óró, you are welcome home! Óró, you are welcome home!

Óró, sé do bheatha 'bhaile! Anois ar theacht an tsamhraidh.
Óró, you are welcome home! Now that the summer is coming

Jig Step Dance Key

General body position: Students should begin the dance with their right foot in front of the left, feet turned out. Their feet should be crossed so that the toes of the left foot touch the right side of the middle of the right foot. A dancer's legs should be straight, and knees should not be bent. Arms are at the side, with fingers in a loose fist. The child's back should be straight, shoulders should be back, head up, and eyes forward. (See appendix for the ethnography recorded at Ina Fitzpatrick's studio. It contains great tricks to help students achieve the correct Irish dancing posture.)

The Jig Step

> Right foot: (The same dance steps are performed first with the right foot in front and then with the left foot in front.)
>
> Step front: The dancer steps forward on right foot and lifts the back foot up behind him or her. If possible he or she should try to aim to kick his bottom with the left foot during this move.
>
> Step back: The dancer steps back on the left foot.
>
> Hop back 2-3-4: The dancer lifts the right leg and brings it back behind the left leg. Then on the 2-3-4 the dancer takes little steps in place (left, right, left). The steps are very little and almost can be seen as a way to shift the weight from one foot to another.

This procedure is repeated one more time as written above. The third time it is slightly different. You do the steps above and then add the two steps below onto the dance.

> Up hop back: The dancer lifts right knee in the air and touches his or her foot to his or her knee before bringing it back behind the left foot.
>
> Hop back 2-3-4: (This is different from the others!) The dancer lifts his or her left leg and brings it behind the right leg to prepare for the left leg of the step.

> Left foot (the steps are the same; just the feet are switched):
>
> Step front: The dancer steps forward on the left foot and lifts the back foot up behind him or her. If possible he or she should try to aim to kick his bottom with the right foot during this move.
>
> Step back: The dancer steps back on the right foot.
>
> Hop back 2-3-4: The dancer lifts his or her left leg and brings it back behind the right leg. Then on the 2-3-4 the dancer takes little steps in place

(right, left, right). The steps are very little and almost can be seen as a way to shift the weight from one foot to another.

This procedure is repeated one more time as written above. The third time you do the steps above and then add the two steps below onto the dance.

Up hop back: The dancer lifts left leg in the air (bent at the knee) and touches his or her foot to his or her knee before bringing it back behind the right foot.

Hop back 2-3-4: (This is different from the others!) The dancer lifts his or her right leg and brings it behind the left leg.

The student stretches his or her right leg straight out in front of him or her, with pointed foot resting on the floor, and takes a bow.

LESSON: 3

Objective: Experiencing the Irish Dance Tradition

Goals:

- Students will understand what step dancing looks like at the semiprofessional or professional level.
- Students will be able to play the first half of the "Milltown Jig" as a class.
- Students will be able to sing the chorus of another song from the Irish tradition.

Standards:

- U.S. National Standards for Music Education:
  - 1b: Students will sing expressively with appropriate dynamics, phrasing, and interpretation.
  - 2c: Echo short rhythms and melodic patterns.
  - 7a: Devise criteria for evaluating performances and compositions.
  - 7b: Explain, using appropriate music terminology, their personal preferences for specific musical works and styles.
  - 9a: Identify by genre or style aural examples of music from various historical periods and cultures.

Materials:

- Class set of tin whistles
- CDs
  - *When I Was Young* by Len Graham, and Garry Ó Briain, Pádraigín Ní Uallacháin (optional)
  - Recorded instrumental selection of the teacher's choice to listen to on the way into class, preferably containing the tin whistle
  - Recording of "Milltown Jig"
- Transcription and accompanying CD (track 3) of "The Fox and the Hare"
- Video or DVD of *Riverdance, Dancing on Dangerous Ground*, or *Lord of the Dance* fast-forwarded to a preselected dance sequence

Transmission process:

1. Introducing the tradition
- The teacher will turn on a recording of Irish music (e.g., Planxty, the Bothy Band) for the students to listen to as they enter the room.

2. Learning the tradition
• The "Milltown Jig" (tin whistle)
  ○ The teacher will begin by reviewing what the students already know.
  ○ The class will play what they already know.
  ○ The teacher will teach the students the last part of the tune.
  ○ The class will play through the whole tune.
  ○ The class will tell the teacher where they feel they are having difficulty, and those portions will be practiced.
  ○ The class will run through the tune one final time.
• Step dancing: learning the jig
  ○ Students will review the left foot of the jig step.
  ○ Students will try dancing the right and left foot together.
  ○ The teacher will give the students time to practice on their own while he or she goes around and corrects any mistakes.
  ○ The class will perform the steps together, with the teacher singing the steps.
  ○ The class will perform the steps with the jig recording, or the teacher will perform it on her own tin whistle.

3. Experiencing the tradition
• At this point, if it is possible, a local step-dance school will come into the class and do a fifteen- to twenty-minute demonstration of soft and hard shoe dancing. The dancers will explain the significance of their dance outfits, shoes, and dances. They will explain how they learned Irish step dancing (where they trained, who trained them, what influenced them). They will also address the competitive aspect of step dancing. In order for their students to qualify for competitions, Irish dance schools must register with the Irish Dance Teachers Association of North America. Before schools are eligible to register with IDTANA, one of their teachers must take and pass the TCRG exam and become a Teagascóir Choimisiúin le Rinci Gaelacha (Commission Certified Irish Dance Teacher). The commission's website is www.idtana.org. Any school in your area would be listed on this site.
• If this is not possible, the students will watch a portion of *Riverdance*, *Dancing on Dangerous Ground*, or *Lord of the Dance*.

4. Discussing the tradition
• The teacher will review what the students learned and allow the questions to be answered either by the step dancers or herself or himself.

5. Closing formulae
- The teacher will end the class by introducing "The Fox and the Hare." This version of the song is a mixture of two different sets of words from Jimmy Crowley, of Cork, and Peg Clancy, County Tipperary.
- The teacher will teach the class the chorus of the song.
- The teacher will sing the song, and the class will join her on the chorus.

Assessment (continuous and noncontinuous)

- The teacher will assess each student's progress on the "Milltown Jig."
- The teacher will assess each student's progress on the jig step.

Teacher reflection

The Fox and The Hare

Transcribed by Rebecca Farrell
Learned from "When I Was Young" by
Len Graham, Garry Ó Briain and
Pádraigín Ní Uallacháin

As I came trot-ting o - ver the hill I spied a fox and he sleep-ing A

cute lit-tle fox and he hi-din in the furze the tops of his two ears a peep - in The

fox and the hare and the bad-ger and the bear the birds in the green-wood trees all the

pre-ty lit-tle rab-bits all en-gag-ing in their hab-its and they're all hav-ing fun but me. Good

mor - row fox good mor - row sir pray what is that your eat - ing a

fine fat goose I stole - from you And will you come and taste it.

2. Oh no indeed bold fox I said
   How dare you boldly taunt me
   I vow and I swear that you'll
      dearly pay
   For the fine fat goose you're eating.

3. Bad cess to you, you bold bad fox
   That stole my geese and ate them.
   My great big drake, my fine fat hen,
   And the nicest little ducks in Erin.

An Madairín Rua (The Little Fox)

Transcribed by Rebecca Farrell
Learned from "When I Was Young" by
Len Graham, Garry Ó Briain and
Pádraigín Ní Uallacháin

Curfa: An ma-dai-ri-n ru-a ru-a ru-a rua - rua   ma-dai-ri-n ru-a ta gran-da

-dai-ri-n ru-a and he hi-din in the furze   the tops of his two ears a peep-in. 1.As

came trot-ting o - ver the hill   I   spied a fox and he ate-ing   A

-te lit-tle fox and he hi-din in the furze   the tops of his two ears a peep-in

ood morrow fox, good morrow Sir,
ray what is that you're ateing
fine fat goose I stole from you
nd will you come and taste it.

Oh no indeed bold fox I said
How dare you boldly taunt me
vow and I swear that you'll dearly pay
For my fine fat goose you're ateing.

LESSON 4

Objective: Introduction to macaronic songs and set dancing

Goals:

- Students will have an understanding of what a macaronic song is.
- Students will be able to successfully dance "Walls of Limerick" with the aid of a caller.
- Students will be able to successfully perform the entire "Milltown Jig" on tin whistle.
- Students will be able to successfully perform the entire jig step with music.

Standards:

- U.S. National Standards for Music Education:
  - 1b: Students will sing expressively with appropriate dynamics, phrasing, and interpretation.
  - 1c: Sing from memory a varied repertoire of songs representing genres and styles from diverse cultures.
  - 7b: Explain, using appropriate music terminology, their personal preferences for specific musical works and styles.
  - 8b: Identify ways in which the principles and subject matter of other disciplines taught in school are interrelated with those of music (history).
  - 9a: Identify by genre or style aural examples of music from various historical periods and cultures.

Materials:

- Music for "Walls of Limerick"
- Class set of tin whistles
- CDs
  - *When I Was Young* by Len Graham, and Gary Ó Briain, Pádraigín Ní Uallacháin (optional)
- Recorded selection of the teacher's choice to listen to on the way into class
- Transcription and accompanying CD of "The Fox and the Hare" (track 3) and "An Maidrín Rua" (track 4)

Transmission process:

1. Introducing the tradition
- The teacher will turn on a recording of Irish music (e.g., recordings by De Danann or Déanta) for the students to listen to as they enter the room. While they listen, the students will describe, using appropriate musical terminology, whether they like the piece or not.

2. Learning the tradition
- "The Fox and the Hare" (song)
  ○ The students will review the song from last week and sing it as a class.
  ○ They will review the story line and make sure that it is clear in their minds.
- The "Milltown Jig" (tin whistle)
  ○ Students will review what they learn.
  ○ Students will play the tune entirely at a steady tempo.
  ○ Any difficulties will be rehearsed.
  ○ The teacher will demonstrate a cut ornamentation and show where it goes in the tune. Students who feel comfortable can add it to their performance.
- Jig step (step dance)
  ○ The step will be reviewed and performed.
  ○ The teacher and a few student volunteers will play the tune while the students dance.
- "Walls of Limerick" (set dance)
  ○ See appendix (Ina Fitzpatrick Ethnography) for the steps. (Another variation of Ina's steps can also be found in the appendix).
  ○ The teacher will pair up the students and guide them to the correct position.
  ○ The teacher will teach the dance one small part at a time, each time adding onto what was previously learned.
  ○ The class will try to dance what they know with the help of the teacher.
  ○ The teacher will put on the music (any reel will do), and the class will dance with the music.
  ○ The class will sit down, and the teacher will talk to them a little about set dancing. She will explain how it has rural origins and that these dances use to be danced at the crossroads. The teacher will explain to the students that these types of dances generally are danced with eight people. They also are named after the area of Ireland where they originated.

3. Discussing the tradition
- The teacher will tell the class he or she h[...] this period. The teacher will tell the class t[...] macaronic song and is in both English and [...] forth between languages is used to create a[...]
- The teacher will sing the song ("An Maidrí[...] tion from the students.
- When the teacher is finished, he or she wil[...] thought. (The students may recognize tha[...] Rua" is the same as "The Fox and the Ha[...] discuss with the students how songs are le[...] This method of transmission results in chang[...] either accidentally or on purpose. As a result[...] multiple versions of the same song.

4. Closing formulae
- The class will sing the curfá of "An Maidrín [...] leave.

Voice

Assessment (continuous and noncontinuous)

- Students will be assessed on their ability to recog[...] even though the words have changed.
- Students will be assessed on their ability to play th[...] the jig.
- Students' progress on "Walls of Limerick" will be[...]

Teacher reflection

LESSON 5

Objective: Introduction to the session and the ceili

Goals:

- Students will have an understanding of the instruments commonly played in a session.
- Students will be able to identify these instruments by sight and sound.
- Students will be able to verbalize the difference between a session and a ceili.
- Students will be able to perform a dance commonly found at ceilis.

Standards:

- U.S. National Standards for Music Education:
  - 2a: Perform (on an instrument) on pitch in rhythm, with appropriate dynamics and timbre, and maintain a steady tempo.
  - 6b: Demonstrate perceptual skills by moving, by answering questions about, and by describing aural examples of music of various styles representing diverse cultures.
  - 6d: Identify the sounds of a variety of instruments, including many orchestra and band instruments, and instruments from various cultures.
  - 9d: Demonstrate audience behavior appropriate for the context and style of music performed.

Materials:

- Suggested recordings of the fiddle, bodhrán, flute, concertina, banjo, and accordion. Other tracks may be substituted if the teacher feels they are more appropriate.
  - "The Blue Idol" on *The Blue Idol* by Altan—outstanding example of the fiddle and the bodhrán
  - "The Big Reel of Ballynacally" on *Sunny Spells and Scattered Showers* by Solas—exceptional example of the banjo and button accordion (referred to frequently as the box)
  - The tracks on any recording by the group Lúnasa—excellent examples of flute playing
  - The Mulcahy family album *Notes from the Heart*—terrific examples of concertina playing on the part of Michelle Mulcahy
- Class set of tin whistles

- Transcription of "Shoo the Donkey" and appropriate music (*Dance Music of Ireland*, vol. 2, track 8, by Matt Cunningham, can be purchased on Amazon)

Transmission process

1. Introducing the tradition
- Students will enter the classroom and be asked to identify the instruments playing when the music stops ("The Big Reel of Ballynacally" by Solas—banjo and button accordion).
- Students will partner up and exchange ideas of the instruments they heard and why they thought that way.
- The class will discuss their answers together, and then the teacher will reveal the correct instruments.
- The teacher will explain what the instruments are and where they can be heard being played in Ireland. The teacher will talk with the students about the instruments and their importance in Irish music.
- Learn about the history of the instrumental tradition (reference previous chapter).
- See pictures of instruments and musicians from the tradition.

2. Learning the tradition
- The "Milltown Jig" (tin whistle)
  ○ Students will collect their whistle from the teacher and sit down in their seats.
  ○ The students will review their tune and will try to play it in its entirety without the assistance of the teacher.
  ○ As students put their instruments away and find a partner, the teacher will play another listening example. The class will discuss what instruments they hear and will be shown pictures of the correct instruments ("The Blue Idol" on *The Blue Idol* by Altan—the fiddle and the bódhran).
- "Shoo the Donkey" (set dance)
  ○ The teacher will begin by having the students line up facing the same direction as the teacher.
  ○ The teacher will show the students the dance steps for the movements up to the first turn. (See the directions following this lesson.) The students will try to do it by themselves.

○ The teacher will then show the students how to turn directions. (Face in to look at your partner and then turn the opposite direction from where you originally were.)

○ The class will try to put together all they know. The partners will not hold hands yet, instead concentrating on the feet. The teacher will sing the steps as the class dances.

○ The teacher will show the class how to hold their partner's hands. The same section will be danced again.

○ The class will learn the next part of the dance.

○ The class will put the whole dance together and all try to sing the steps and dance them.

○ The teacher will explain how the dance fits with a particular piece of music. The teacher will tell the students that while they dance "Shoo the Donkey," they need to listen very carefully to the music because the tempo will speed up.

○ The class will listen to the music and quietly sing the steps to themselves. The teacher should refer to the transcription of "Shoo the Donkey" for the appropriate tune to accompany the dance.

○ The class will dance "Shoo the Donkey" together.

3. Discussing the tradition
• The teacher will talk about the differences between a session and a ceili.
   ○ Differences to discuss are how musicians in sessions sit in a circle to play, while in the ceili they generally sit in a line. When musicians get together in sessions, their purpose is to play music together just for music's sake, while the ceili musicians are accompanying dancing. Also, sessions can be very small or very large, while ceilis tend to include many musicians. Finally, sessions are generally located at the local pub, while ceilis occur in a large room like a church hall, school, or other hall of that type.
   ○ Additional reading that pertains to this topic can be found in *Field Guide to the Irish Music Session* by Barry Foy.
• The teacher will talk with the class about their upcoming ceili and answer any questions the students might have.

4. Closing formulae
• Students will write a paragraph or two about what they learned today. If they would prefer to draw, that too would be appropriate.

Assessment (continuous and noncontinuous)

- Students' responses will be observed to see if they have an understanding of the material presented today.
- The teacher will observe the students dancing and determine if they are able to complete the dance and tune.

This lesson could be conducted in one of two ways. For example, the teacher could introduce the instruments to the whole class all at once. This way the teacher would control the information the students were receiving through their listening, and any questions could immediately be answered. Another way to approach this lesson is to have each instrument function as an individual listening station for a small group of students. Additionally, there could be a station to read about how sessions and ceilis function. Students could pair off or be in groups of three, depending on class size, and travel between the eight stations (six for instruments and then one for sessions and one for ceilis). Students would then be able to experience each instrument, see a picture of it, and read a little bit about its role in the session. I have chosen to outline this particular lesson in the more traditional manner of full class discussion due to the lack of space in this book and a desire to make the information I am presenting accessible to as many people as possible. This would not be the case if I created a lesson that was based upon having certain technical resources that are not available to all schools.

Teacher reflection

Shoo the Donkey

Music: Versa Vienna

Positioning: Dancers need to form lines of two. The gentleman's right arm is around the lady's waist, and her left arm is on his right shoulder.

Bars:

A. Advance

8   a. Hop 1 (right step), hop 2 (step with left foot), hop 1-2, hop 1-2, turn and stamp (left). At the same time as the turn, the man puts his left arm around the lady's waist, and the woman puts her right arm on the gentleman's left shoulder. [4 bars]

        b. The movements are repeated on the opposite leg in the opposite direction. The turn will bring the dancers back to face the original direction. [4 bars]

8   Repeat a and b.

B. Hop 1-2

8   Hop 1-2, turn and stamp. Hop 1-2, turn and stamp. Repeat six more times

C. Repeat

Repeat A and B as many times as necessary. The music will get progressively faster until it finishes.

Memory aid:

When I was taught this dance, I was taught a song that went with it to help the dancers remember when to turn. It fits with the tune and is as follows:

A. Advance:

a. Shoo the donkey, shoo the donkey, shoo the donkey and turn (stamp),
b. Shoo the donkey, shoo the donkey, shoo the donkey and turn,
a. Shoo the donkey, shoo the donkey, shoo the donkey and turn (stamp),
b. Shoo the donkey, shoo the donkey, shoo the donkey and turn.

B. Hop 1-2

Shoo the donkey and turn, shoo the donkey and turn,
Shoo the donkey and turn, shoo the donkey and turn,

Shoo the donkey and turn, shoo the donkey and turn,
Shoo the donkey and turn, shoo the donkey and turn.

C. Repeat

Notes on dance terminology:

1. A bar is equivalent to one count of three (1, 2, 3)
2. As the dancers hop on their right and step 1-2 or right-left, they are moving forward. Dancers will make a half turn to face the opposite direction. Dancers should turn in toward their partner.

LESSON 6

Objective: Introduction to the imagined Ireland

Goals:

- Introduce students to the Irish harp and the role it played in Irish history.
- Introduce students to Thomas Moore's melodies and the imagined Ireland.

Standards:

- U.S. National Standards for Music Education:
  - 1a: Sing independently, on pitch and in rhythm, with appropriate timbre, diction, and posture, and maintain a steady tempo.
  - 1b: Sing expressively with appropriate dynamics, phrasing, and interpretation.
  - 1c: Sing from memory a varied repertoire of songs representing genres and styles from diverse cultures.
  - 2a: Perform (on an instrument) on pitch in rhythm, with appropriate dynamics and timbre, and maintain a steady tempo.
  - 6b: Demonstrate perceptual skills by moving, by answering questions about, and by describing aural examples of music of various styles representing diverse cultures.
  - 6d: Identify the sounds of a variety of instruments, including many orchestra and band instruments, and instruments from various cultures.
  - 7b: Explain, using appropriate music terminology, their personal preferences for specific musical works and styles.
  - 8b: Identify ways in which the principles and subject matter of other disciplines taught in the school are interrelated with those of music.
  - 9a: Identify by genre or style aural examples of music from various historical periods and cultures.

Materials:

- Class set of tin whistles
- Recording of an Irish harpist (e.g., Laoise Kelly, Gráinne Yeats)
- Recording of Moore's melodies ("Believe Me If All Those Endearing Young Charms," which can be found on John McDermott's recording *Ireland*)

- Transcription of "Believe Me If All Those Endearing Young Charms" and the accompanying CD (track 5)
- Transcription, accompanying CD (track 6), and game sheet for "I Am the Master" and "Dusty Bluebells" as learned from Sandra Joyce

Transmission process:

1. Introducing the tradition
- Students will enter the classroom and listen to modern or traditional harp music. (If the teacher would like to use traditional harp music written in the old style, then anything composed by Turlough Carolan would be appropriate.)
- The teacher will explain the significance of the harp throughout the history of Ireland. (In addition to its musical importance, the harp has had political significance as well. The harp can be found on Irish euro coins, all government buildings, and official Irish government documents.)
- The students will listen to the piece again.

2. Learning the tradition
- "I Am the Master"/"Dusty Bluebells" (the Irish-American connection)
  - Students will learn how to sing "I Am the Master"/"Dusty Bluebells." (This singing game is very popular among Irish children. This song is intimately connected with the custom in Devonshire and elsewhere of "crying the neck." The "master of the harvest" had his neck adorned with choice wheat grains, or in this case apples are supposed to be used. The festival from which this game comes occurs when the little apples are on the trees and the dusty bluebells are in bloom.)
  - The students will be taught the game that accompanies the song.
  - The students will play the game and sing the song.
- "Believe Me If All Those Endearing Young Charms"
  - The teacher will explain who Thomas Moore was. (See www.pbs.org/ wnet/ihas/composer/moore.html or *Thomas Moore the Poet: His Life and Works* by Andrew James Symington.)
  - The teacher will talk about Moore's melodies. (He wrote poems based on Irish themes that were then set to popular Irish tunes at the time. He wrote this music for the Protestant middle class, to be played for social gatherings held in the home. Hence, it became known as "parlor music.") For more information, consult the previous chapter.
  - The teacher will explain to the students how these poems were created to imagine a free Ireland like it once existed prior to the English. This idea of Ireland prior to the English was greatly romanticized and far from the actual truth.

- The teacher will play a recording of "Believe Me If All Those Endearing Young Charms."
- The class will discuss what the words mean and the story behind the song.

3. Discussing the tradition
- The teacher will facilitate a discussion about the "Irishness" of Thomas Moore's melodies. The students will be asked to decide which type of Irish music they prefer and why.

4. Closing formulae
- The students will be asked to write briefly about what they learned today prior to lining up.

Assessment (continuous and noncontinuous)

- The students will be assessed on their participation in class today.

Teacher reflection

Believe Me, If All Those Endearing Young Charms

Transcribed by Rebecca Farrell
Lyrics by Thomas Moore
Traditional Irish Air

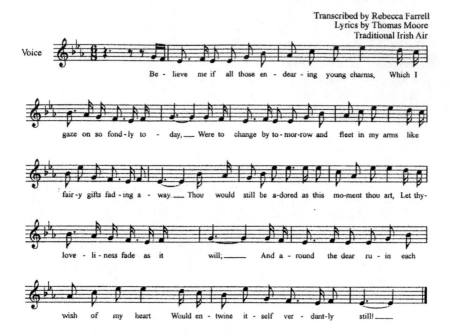

Voice

Be - lieve me if all those en - dear - ing young charms, Which I

gaze on so fond-ly to - day, Were to change by to-mor-row and fleet in my arms like

fair-y gifts fad - ing a - way. Thou would still be a-dored as this mo-ment thou art, Let thy-

love - li - ness fade as it will; And a - round the dear ru - in each

wish of my heart Would en - twine it - self ver - dant-ly still!

2. It is not while beauty and youth are thine own,
And thy cheeks unprofaned by a tear,
That the ferver and faith of a soul can be known,
To which time will but make thee more dear,
No the heart that has truly loved never forgets,
But as truly loves on to the close,
As the sunflower turns on her god when he sets,
The same look which she'd turned when he rose.

I Am The Master/Dusty Bluebells

Transcribed by Rebecca Farrell
Traditional Irish Song

"I Am the Master"/"Dusty Bluebells"

Game directions: A ring is formed, but the children do not catch hands, merely letting the arms hang at the side. A leader is chosen, who walks to the time of the music in and out through the others until the words "I am the master" are sung, when the leader stops and taps the shoulders of the nearest player. The person tapped follows the leader, and the game goes on until all have left the ring and are walking in single file to the music, and all tapping the shoulders of the player in front, when the second verse is being sung.

LESSON 7

Objective: The old and new tradition

Goals:

- Students will understand the differences that exist between traditional Irish music and popular Irish music today.
- Students will review all they have learned in this unit.

Standards:

- U.S. National Standards for Music Education:
  - ○ 1a: Sing independently, on pitch and in rhythm, with appropriate timbre, diction, and posture, and maintain a steady tempo.
  - ○ 1b: Sing expressively with appropriate dynamics, phrasing, and interpretation.
  - ○ 1c: Sing from memory a varied repertoire of songs representing genres and styles from diverse cultures.
  - ○ 2a: Perform (on an instrument) on pitch in rhythm, with appropriate dynamics and timbre, and maintain a steady tempo.
  - ○ 3c: Improvising simple rhythmic variations and simple melodic embellishments on familiar melodies. (This standard can be used with advanced instrumentalists. In this situation the "Milltown Jig" can be arranged into a large ensemble piece using the same procedure that Denis Liddy uses with his ceili band in chapter 3.)
  - ○ 7b: Explain, using appropriate music terminology, their personal preferences for specific musical works and styles.

Materials:

- Class set of tin whistles
- A CD of the group the Corrs
- Transcription of "The Rattlin' Bog" (found in *The Music Connection Grade 3*)

Transmission process:

1. Introducing the tradition
- Students will come into the room, where a Corrs CD will be playing.
- The students will discuss if this music is traditional or not and why.

2. Learning the tradition
- "The Rattlin' Bog" (song)
  - ○ Students will learn a very traditional song that is taught to Irish children in schools today.
  - ○ The teacher will sing the students the refrain to the song and ask them to join in.
  - ○ The teacher will sing the song again, and this time the students are welcome to join in on the entire piece.
- The "Milltown Jig" (tin whistle)
  - ○ The students will review the tune on the whistle several times.

3. Experiencing the tradition
- If musicians are available to visit the classroom, then this section of the class would provide the teacher with the opportunity to allow it to happen.
  Questions for the musician(s):
  - ○ When did you begin playing?
  - ○ How were you taught to play your instrument?
  - ○ What other musicians influenced your own personal musical style?
  - ○ If you are just starting to play Irish music, what musicians would you recommend listening to?
  - ○ Do you ever play for a ceili or session?
  - ○ How do you know when to add ornamentation to a tune?
  - ○ How do you play ornamentations?
  - ○ What terminology should you know when you are listening to or discussing Irish music?
- If an Irish musician is unable to come into the classroom, most touring Irish bands will have video performances posted on their websites. The band Outside Track also has a video interview on their website where they discuss how the band came together and what their influences are and the band's approach to arranging Irish music.

4. Discussing the tradition
- The teacher will review with the students what they have learned in class during this unit.

5. Closing formulae
- The students will create invitations for the ceili. The families will be invited to attend.

Assessment (continuous and noncontinuous)

- The teacher will listen to each student play the "Milltown Jig" to determine the student's proficiency on the tune.

Teacher reflection

LESSONS 8, 9, 10

Objective: To prepare for the ceili. During weeks eight through ten, class time will be used to review and practice for the ceili.

Ceili program ideas:

- Storytelling: students will tell the story of Ireland's history and what they learned during the unit.
- Each class will take a turn at singing one of the songs it learned during the unit. If it is Christmastime, and the school districts will allow it, the ceili will begin with the singing of the Wexford Carol (accompanying CD track 7), which will be taught during weeks eight through ten.
- Half the students will perform "Walls of Limerick" at the beginning of the ceili, and the other half will do it later on.
- Students who are proficient at the "Milltown Jig" will perform the tune.
- The classes will be divided in half, and one half of the grade will perform the jig step they learned.
- All the parents will learn "Shoo the Donkey" and will dance with their children.
- Children will all sing "The Rattlin' Bog," with the parents joining in on the chorus.

Potential program:

- Irish and American national anthems are performed.
- Teacher introduces the purpose of a ceili.
- Wexford Carol is sung by all the children.
- Half the grade performs "Walls of Limerick."
- Story about the use of the Irish language is read by the students.
- One class will sing a song ("Óró Sé Do Bheatha 'Bhaile") with the help of the teacher.
- Half the students will perform the jig step
- A child will talk about songs that tell stories.
- One of the classes will sing "My Aunt Jane."
- One of the students will talk about the instruments used in the Irish musical tradition.
- One of the classes will sing "The Fox and the Hare."
- "Shoo the Donkey" is danced (with parents).

Break (cookies and juice)

- One class performs "An Maidrín Rua."
- Students talk about how Irish music is learned.
- The other half of students perform the jig step.
- Students sing "I Am the Master"/"Dusty Bluebells."
- Half the grade performs "Walls of Limerick."
- Whole grade sings "The Rattlin' Bog."
- Acknowledgments!

The Wexford Carol

Transcribed by Rebecca Farrell
Traditional Irish Carol

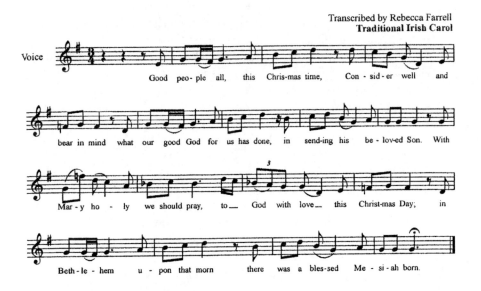

2. The night before the happy tide,
The noble Virgin and her guide
Were long time seeking up and down
To find a lodging in the town.
But mark how all things come to pass;
From ev'ry door repell'd alas!
As long foretold their refuge all
Was but an humble ox's stall.

3. Near Bethlehem did shepherds keep
Their flocks of lambs and feeding sheep;
To whom God's angels did appear,
Which put the shepherds in great fear,
"Prepare to go," the angels said,
"To Bethlehem, be not afraid;
For there you'll find, this happy morn.
A princely babe, sweet Jesus born."

4. With thankful heart and joyful mind,
The shepherds went the babe to find,
And as God's angel had foretold,
They did our Saviour Christ behold,
Within a manger he was laid,
And by his side the virgin maid,
Attending on the Lord of life,
Who came on earth to end all strife.

Conclusion

I think the music came from Ireland because it sounds like you can do Irish step dancing to it.

—Lydia, age nine

In the past, the United States has been referred to as a melting pot, blending all races and creeds into one view of what it meant to be American. Today, that view has changed. The United States of America has become a patchwork quilt, striving, as best it can, to respect and embrace the differences that make it colorful. In particular, there has been renewed recognition of the Irish as an ethnic group within the United States. This development has resulted in the desire of Irish Americans to reconnect with their roots. My parents, both of Irish descent, were part of that movement. As I grew up in the 1990s, my family engrained in me a sense of pride about my Irish heritage. As a result, when I began to teach elementary general music, the limited resources available to those of us who wished to "pass on" the tradition frustrated me. It was this frustration that pushed me to cross the water to Ireland in September 2005. Ethnomusicology promised me a chance to study Irish music in its cultural context, and I was intrigued.

Ireland's traditional music is a living and growing genre that is historically rurally based and constructed around certain customs that accompany such lifestyles. While traditional musicians generally teach small groups of children privately, the attempt to integrate this cultural art form into the national schools has slightly altered this approach. From my research I was able to highlight the similarities in the method of transmission used by teachers in large classroom situations both within and outside the national schools. From these observations and my ethnographic research in the United States I was able to develop a unit on traditional Irish music for American third grade music students. I believe the lessons contained in this unit demonstrate my understanding and respect for the tradition. It is my hope that these lessons will be used in other music classrooms to introduce children of all ages to the beautiful and exciting music and dances that belong to the Irish music tradition.

According to John Blacking (2000, p. 4), "Ethnomusicology has the power to create a revolution in the world of music and education if it follows the implication of its discoveries and develops as a method and not merely an area of study." When I first read that line in *How Musical Is Man?* (Blacking, 2000) I was struck by how extreme it was. After completing a master's degree in this discipline, I have a better idea of what Blacking was aiming for when he made that statement. Although I do not feel that ethnomusicology will incite the revolution that Blacking, a Marxist, hoped it would, I do have to agree that ethnomusicology has the ability to change the way one looks at the world and the manners in which people interact in their environment. The ethnomusicology program at University of Limerick opened me up to new ways of thinking and new approaches to living life. I feel that my study directly affects my interaction with others and has had a profound effect on my approach to creating world music lessons. In that respect, ethnomusicology has created a revolution, and I know I will spend many years to come reaping the benefits from it.

Appendix

- Excerpts from Interview with Dr. John O'Flynn
- Excerpts from Denis Liddy Ethnography
- Excerpts from Ina Fitzpatrick Ethnography
- Additional Lesson Material
  - Lesson Format
  - Milltown Jig Transcriptions
  - Tin Whistle Ornamentation Guide
  - Other Irish Traditional Music and Dance Resources

EXCERPTS FROM INTERVIEW WITH DR. JOHN O'FLYNN

Interview: Dr. John O'Flynn
Interview Date: November 2, 2005
Interview Time: 5:00 PM
Interview Location: The Allegro Café at the University of Limerick
Conditions: The café itself was empty, but the employees were cleaning up
   for the day, and as a result it was very noisy.
Present: Rebecca E. Farrell and Dr. John O'Flynn
Language: English

Interview:	Side A
JO:	So you want to know about the status of traditional music in the curriculum in Ireland, primarily the primary curriculum? So the first thing I should say to you is that it is not widely practiced. There are two senses of the word "curriculum," obviously one in which people think of the document and so on, and the most recent revision to the national curriculum for primary school was in 1999 and you can get that—
REF:	The orange one, right? (JO: Yes, so you have it?) Noel Lennon is in our class, and he gave me his copy. So I have read through the document, but it is one of those things where it is assumed you have certain knowledge about how the curriculum is set up, which I don't, since I am coming from the States.
JO:	Noel is practicing in the primary school, is that right? Yeah, he was a student of our college. What you will find in the curriculum is that it is organized very similarly to other programs like in North America, Europe, and Australia where you have three strands: performing, composing, and listening. Those would be your three major areas. And within those there are certainly content recommendations, say, for traditional performing groups, and that might be one of the main areas where you would have application of traditional music, but that would be only in some schools.

Probably the most common way is to learn Irish traditional style of playing tin whistle. In my own experience years ago from teaching that would be teaching people in groups. It could be done by a number of methods—by ear, using notation, by *sol–fa*—I have even seen people use the notation created by Rousseau, where he took the numbering. There are two types of teachers teaching tin whistle. One would be a person who is a general music graduate who can teach the children very well but who is not necessarily a traditional musician. That person |

would be very much linked to the school band where they are playing Irish tunes but not necessarily in a traditional style. They would have whistles, piano, accordion, and drums, that kind of basic school band at the primary school. And then less common would be to have teachers in the schools who themselves are quite advanced traditional musicians, and they are teaching in a much more community type of style. In that situation they might have a lot of support for music in the primary school system, and they would have small class meetings, and the teacher would encourage children to play different instruments, and they would all learn the tunes. In the vast majority of schools the only Irish music that is performed at all is singing. Just bear that in mind. Listening is found in the curriculum, and I think that as a music educator I would encourage people to use listening an awful lot; there is an embedded tradition of using classical music recording only in terms of listening. So that is an emerging area of using traditional music in the classroom. It is still kind of new because I think people are used to using program music like Saint-Saëns, and they don't know quite what to do in classroom practice when listening to jigs and reels and so on. Composing, again I think this is an area lacking in the curriculum. While there is nothing stopping people having composing and improvising in traditional music, most of the composing activities are inspired by Paynter's avant-garde approach to classroom composition, where people approach things through musical concepts and musical elements.* And I am not aware of a huge amount of composing going on even where traditional music is performed. Most of the composing tends to be the avant-garde principle of composition, as opposed to composing in a particular idiom or style.

REF: Now with the singing that you talked briefly about, would the children be learning certain songs? I saw that there were certain suggested songs in the curriculum.

JO: There are no prescribed songs in the primary school (REF: OK.); in secondary school that changes a bit, but in primary school there is none. So prior to the curriculum in 1999 there was an actual directory of songs in Irish; it was actually written "that songs in the Irish language should be given its pride and place"—a direct quote, that was in the 1971 curriculum, which was effectively the curriculum until the new one in 1999. So there is a lot of concern about that part. The use of Irish music is very much on a regional basis; you could have schools in some cities

*British composer and educator John Paynter. According to O'Flynn, Paynter is perhaps best known for his book *Sound and Silence*.

or regions of the country where there [are] no Irish songs in the English or Irish language included. Conversely you could have a school where a lot of ballad singing is done. For example in East Galway there is a large mummer population, so there would be school plays based on the mumming tradition. These plays would include ballads sung in the English language . . . but, again in Gaelic-speaking areas there would be some traditional singing of Irish songs in the Irish language at the school. One of the problems that music educators find with Irish material is that the music education methods tend to be written with adults in mind. They have adult ranges, with very complex rhythms, tonality and so on, and they are really only developing now resources of Irish songs specifically for children.

REF: What resources are preservice primary school teachers given to teach Irish music?

JO: We have four hundred people a year in our college. They would be preparing for everything in the curriculum. The average primary school teacher would have about forty hours of music over the whole degree. In that time they would be expected to cover the key areas of composing, listening, and performing. Most of the performing would comprise of singing. It would comprise certainly of the percussion instruments available in primary schools. We don't have the ability to teach people instruments in groups, because with four hundred people we don't have the resources. But it is a worry, to be honest. They would certainly have in the listening section a quarter of what they studied would be traditional, or traditionally derived music. And what I mean by traditional is the instruments of a tradition or crossover groups. In the singing repertoire we would go quite internationally, there would be a number of songs that would be from Ireland but that wouldn't be taught exclusively.

REF: So there is a set repertoire list that preservice teachers learn?

JO: It varies from college to college. I can only speak about Limerick, but we do prepare 40 percent of the primary school teachers in the country. What we do is we publish an in-house songbook of about fifty songs from all over the world—not with the aim of being all over the world, but just songs we feel are good to use in classroom practice. We work with materials, but we don't prescribe to teachers what they do and don't do. These are materials that the lecturers like to use, they recommend, and use in workshops.

REF: Is it possible that at some point I could come see a lecture?

JO: Yeah, sure, of course.

EXCERPTS FROM DENIS LIDDY ETHNOGRAPHY

Ethnographer: Rebecca E. Farrell

Teacher: Denis Liddy, Barefield National School teacher and traditional musician. Liddy is from County Clare, Ireland, and his fiddle playing is representative of that style. An accomplished musician, he has recorded several CDs and can be seen performing frequently throughout Ireland and the United States.

Location: Barefield Community Center

Date: March 2, 2006

Time: 3:00–3:30 PM

Event: Under-12 (9- to 12-year-old) Barefield Ceili Band rehearsal

DL: OK, so we are going to pick up where we left off last week with the hornpipe. We were starting to make some arrangements of it. So let's see how it goes. [To me DL says, "Obviously we need to practice the part we did last week, but this will give you an idea of how we basically go about arranging a piece."] I think we had box start us with a drone, and then the fiddles started after four with a drone and flutes start after three. It's a bit confusing at the start. [Tuning occurs.] Let's try that and see how it goes. Ready? One, two three . . .

Box: D drone	A drone	G drone	A drone	G drone
Fiddle 1 2 3 4	E drone	D drone	E drone	D drone
Flute: 1 2 3 E–D–C$^{\#}$	A–A–B–C$^{\#}$–A	D–B–B–A–B	E–D–C$^{\#}$–A–A–B–C–A	B–G–G–F$^{\#}$–G

Box: A drone		G drone	A drone	G drone	A drone
Fiddle E drone		D drone	E drone	D drone	E drone
Flute: E–D–C$^{\#}$–A–A–B–C$^{\#}$–A		D–B–B–A–B	E–D–C$^{\#}$–E	D–B–G–B	A–A–G–A

Second time through the tune the concertinas join the flute on the tune, fiddle and box keep the drone. (When Denis instructs students on a tune, he sings the note names to them, and as a result I transcribed all the music contained in this lesson in the same manner.) The second half of the tune is then picked up by the concertinas. Unfortunately all but one or two of the children have had a memory slip and forget to come in. Denis stops the group to try to sort out what happened. He quickly realizes that the concertinas are spread out throughout the ensemble and need to sit next to one another for support. Without wasting any time he moves the different instruments into their proper sections and asks the students to remember to always sit in those places each week. By now there are ten fiddle players, four flutists, four box players, four concertina players, and one harpist. Once the ensemble is sorted, Denis has the concertinas run through their solo, which is the next part of the tune.

DL: OK, concertinas, your solo, one, two, three, four . . .

Concertinas: A–B–C$^{\#}$–D–E E–F$^{\#}$–G–D–E A–B–C$^{\#}$–D–E–E–D–G–D–B–G A–B–C$^{\#}$–D–E E–F$^{\#}$–G–D–E–D–C$^{\#}$–E–D–B–G–B–A–A–G–A

The second time practicing this tune goes better than the first run-through, but the students are still not sure of their part. To help them with the melody, Denis sings the beginning of the solo. The group continues on with the arrangement, and the fiddles join the concertinas on the second round of the second half of the tune.

DL: [He stops the ensemble.] Let's try that again. Will you three
                       [gesturing to the older fiddle players] play with the concertinas?
                       [Students nod.] Grand. OK, let's run through it again.

Students run the hornpipe to that point. Flutes continue with their turn to solo on the second half of the tune. Denis adds a box player on a drone during this section of the piece. The flutes continue to solo when they return to the first part of the tune (E–D–C$^{\#}$). The repeat of this section features the flutes and fiddles, with the box playing the drone from the beginning. Everyone joins in on playing the second half of the tune two times in unison.

DL: [He waits until the piece finishes.] At that end part, three things
                       need to occur: number one, you all have to play together; number
                       two, the melody still needs to be heard; and number three, the
                       tune needs to be played, the first part twice and the second part
                       twice. When you have the melody you can add something, but it
                       still needs to be heard. OK, so listen to the overall picture of the
                       piece. You may only have one color, a little red or a little blue,
                       but they all have to fit into the overall color of the piece. Let's
                       talk it through. We are starting with the drone in the bass, then
                       one, two, three, the flutes and the fiddles come in after four with
                       your drone. That's the first part. Then what happens next?
STUDENT: Concertinas take the melody.
DL: Right. Then the second time the flutes. Then we go back and
                       we will change it on the second time through; the harp, Leah on

fiddle, and Andy on flute will join in. Anyone lost? No? OK, let's try it.

Students begin, but the fiddles come in on the wrong beat.

DL:	OK, remember, flutes, come in on three, and fiddles come in on . . .
STUDENTS:	Four.
DL:	OK, right. Let's try it again.
DL:	[Waits until after the students make it through the entire arrangement.] OK, that's not too bad. Fiddles need to practice the tune in their lower octave. [He fixes a few note problems in the different sections of the tune.] OK, let's look at the "Heel and Toe Polka." All right, let's try to run it. What do I mean by that? I mean let's run the first part twice and the second part twice. One, two, three, four . . .

Students run the tune.
All instruments:

First part:
$F^\#$–G–A–A–B–A–$F^\#$'–$F^\#$'
E–$F^\#$'–G'–B–E–D–$C^\#$'–B–A
$F^\#$–G–A–A–B–A–$F^\#$'–$F^\#$'
E–$F^\#$'–G'–B–E–D–D'

Second part:
B–C–D–G'–B–C–B–A–G–A–B
C–B–A–B–C–D–E–D–D
B–C–D–G'–B–C–B–A–G–A–B
C–B–A–B–C–$F^\#$'–A–G–G

DL:	Now that was fine. Just watch the second part. The first part has a C . . . [long pause]
STUDENT:	Sharp.
DL:	And the second part changes to . . . [long pause] what does it change to?
STUDENT:	Natural.
DL:	Right. Some of you are forgetting to put the C-sharp in the first part. Just make sure you watch that. OK, let's try to arrange that for a second. Flute, fiddle, and box and concertina, the four of you start it off just to see how it sounds. OK, try it, one, two, three, four . . .

The four older students play the tune together in unison.

DL: OK, right. Umm . . . the four boxes, do you got the tune? [Students say yes.] Right. Four boxes, let's try the second part. One, two, three . . .

Four box players begin playing the second part

DL: OK, can anyone hear what is happening? Does anyone hear what is happening, or is it just me?

STUDENT: There is a difference in sound because the in and the out of the bellows is messy.

DL: Right, is there anything else that is happening?

STUDENT: They are not together. They are rushing.

DL: OK, boxes, let's try to play the first part. One, two, three, four . . .

The box players play the first part together

DL: That was better that time. Just watch your rhythm. [He sings the first half of the first part of the tune to demonstrate the correct rhythm.] The first part is long, and the second part is short. OK, flutes, second part please. One, two, three . . .

Flutes jump right in. (Andy, the oldest flute player, leads the group.)

DL: OK, that's fine. Just watch the C-naturals. All right fiddles, can you try the second part with the flutes please? One, two, three . . .

Flutes and fiddles play together. (There is a little bit of a disagreement in tempo occurring.)

DL: OK. [He borrows a fiddle from a student and plays the tune with chords underneath it. Students sit quietly and wait for the next direction.] Louise, can you give me a D and A, please? [Student plays the drone, while Denis plays the melody over the top. He stops.] Can you give me an A and an F-sharp? Do you have an F-sharp? How about an A and a high F-sharp [$F^{#'}$]? How about an A and D? [Student tries all combinations.] When I get to this note, can you play an A and D, and then when I get to this note play an A and a high F-sharp? [Denis plays and Louise plays the drone.]

Denis on fiddle: $F^{#}$–G–A–A–B–A–$F^{#}$–$F^{#}$–E–$F^{#}$–G

Louise on box: D+A A+F$^{\#}$'

DL: OK? Fiddles, do you want to play the first part? And the box is in the first part. That's grand. Fiddles and flutes, play the first part, but not too fast. Louise, can you possibly play those drones in the first part? One, two, three . . .

Students play it all together. Denis cues the box.

DL: OK, right, so we are going to work on that next week. From now on you may be stuck on your own now and again. I am going to ask you play with the box or the harp. I am going to try to get to hear as many people individually as possible. Not knowing the tune is not an excuse. You have the CDs, so you need to listen to them and practice with them. Well, that's it, see you Tuesday.

Under-12 Ceili Band Rehearsal Lesson Plan

Purpose: To review the hornpipe that had been arranged last week.
To arrange the "Heel and Toe Polka" for the ceili band.

Transmission process:
Step 1: Teacher greets students.
Step 2: Teacher informs students of what they are going to begin with that day.
Step 3: Teacher highlights who will begin the piece and counts the group off.
Step 4: Teacher stops the students when the ensemble gets confused.
Step 5: Teacher reorganizes the ensemble into sections.
Step 6: Teacher rehearses the concertinas on their solo. He cues the rest of the group to join in at the appropriate time.
Step 7: Teacher stops groups and adds older, stronger players to the concertina solo. Start from that spot again.
Step 8: Teacher reviews what needs to occur at the end of the second run-through where all the instruments are playing in unison.
Step 9: Teacher reviews what happens throughout the entire arrangement. Students are asked to help explain how the arrangement is constructed.
Step 10: Teacher gives everyone the cue to begin playing. The flutes come in at the wrong time, and everyone must start again.
Step 11: Teacher comments on the performance. Then he tells the students the next piece that they are going to practice. It is the "Heel and Toe Polka." He asks the students to run the whole piece. Before they do this,

he reviews what running a piece means. (All play the first part twice and then all play the second part twice.)

Step 12: Teacher comments on the performance and fixes mistakes (C-sharp vs. C-natural).

Step 13: Teacher arranges the tune.

Step 14: Teacher asks for student input on why mistakes are occurring.

Step 15: Students fix the mistakes and try to play another section of the tune.

Step 16: Teacher arranges the next section, and the students play it.

Step 17: Teacher experiments with different drone possibilities.

Step 18: Students play what they have so far.

Step 19: Teacher wraps up the class with practice instructions.

EXCERPTS FROM INA FITZPATRICK ETHNOGRAPHY

Ethnographer: Rebecca E. Farrell

Teacher: Ina Fitzpatrick, Irish step-dancing teacher. Fitzpatrick was born and raised in Cahirciveen, County Kerry, Ireland, and began dancing as a small child. She started a teaching studio six years ago. During the week she travels to the national schools in the area and teaches set dances to all the students. During the weeknights and on Saturday morning she teaches classes out of the studio at her house.

Location: Cahirciveen, County Kerry, Ireland

Date: March 5, 2006

Time: 11:00 AM to 12:30 PM

Event: Group beginner and advance beginner step-dancing lessons. Students are between the ages of four and nine.

IF:	OK, when you are ready, girls, line up and we'll start with our warm-ups. Shauna, you come to this side of me darling. Have you all enough room? OK, and mind that your toes aren't turned in. And so we'll start with our marching. One, two, three, four . . . [Students begin marching.] And left, left, left.
IF:	And ready, right (point), left, right, left. Point the toe as you march, everybody stretching. And the right hand and left hand. [Students stretch them to the side and over.] And two hands [to beat of the music, which is a jig]. . . . A way up, a way up, we're pointing all the time. Stretching. March time again. Nicely, don't hit your feet on the floor. Make a fist and put them at your sides and kick up behind and kick and kick. [Students kick their feet up to hit their bum; this is a move they will use in step-dancing class.] And march! And bring your knee up and point your toe. March time again. Now, point [right] and touch, point and touch, make sure you have your toe pointed! Now left leg! Point and stretch your toe in front, stretch your toe behind! Mark time again. Now we are going to reach out and stretch your toe in front. Left [point], [feet] together, right, together, left together, right together. We are going to swing the arms and point, and point, and point and point, and point, point, and point, and mark time again. And good job, everybody! [These warm-ups are different from the ones I saw briefly during the three-to-five-year-old class. There the basics of Irish step dancing were taught through games and rhymes like "Palms out, hide Mr. Thumb, arms at the side. The magic string pulls your head up, and you have two really heavy shoulders."]

IF: Now everyone get in her lines for 1-2-3s [one-two-threes]. [Students scurry to create three lines facing the mirrors.] OK, here we go, 1-2-3, 2-2-3, 3-2-3, 4-2-3. [The first students begin with their 1-2-3s at the front of the line and by the 4-2-3s is at the back of the line. The other students, continually doing 1-2-3s as well, have moved up a position. Ina corrects timing and positioning as they go. She pulls out students that need individual help.] Keep your thumbs back. That's better! Turn out your feet and point your toes! Mind the hands! Mind your timing there! One, two, three, keep time, Terrin! Give yourselves a big hand now, well done!

IF: Now we'll make up the sets for the "Walls of Limerick." The big girls take the small girls. Do you want to go together? Two facing two. Becky, would you like to do the "Walls of Limerick"? Here, you go with Becky, and Mikayla you go with me. OK, remember, ladies on the right, gents on the left. Now so, brilliant! This is the dance we did for the St. Patrick's Day parade. All of the bigger children took the smaller children, and it was really lovely with them all dancing together. [Ina did this so that the bigger children could guide the younger ones, who as a general rule are less sure of the dance.] Now! [Music starts—polka and then reel.]

Dance One: "Walls of Limerick"—Four-Hand Set Dance

In 2-3 and bow, back 2-3, back 2-3. In 2-3 and bow, back 2-3, back 2-3 (advance and retire). Ladies change. (Do sevens to the left over to the other lady's position; once in the correct spot they do back 2-3, back 2-3. Then the gents change positions, doing sevens to the right and then 1-2-3s in place. The timing is ladies 1-2-3-4-5-6-7, back 2-3, back 2-3, gents immediately following 1-2-3-4-5-6-7, back 2-3, back 2-3.) Now, grab the opposite hand! (Gents grab opposite lady's hand and dance outward seven, dance two 1-2-3s, and then dance back to their spot, 1-2-3-4-5-6-7, and turn to face their partner on their 1-2-3s.) Now all the way around. (Partners grab hands and dance around the other couple, ending up in the other couple's position facing the opposite direction.) Dance repeats.

IF: [Music stops] Well done! Give yourself a round of applause. All the girls who have led around side step and swing and back step, line up right next to each other right now. [Beginner step.]

The majority of the girls line up, and Ina puts on a reel.

IF: Are we all ready to go? All together first, and then we will go one at a time. Now feet together, point your toes. Hide your thumb, make a fist, heavy shoulders, ready and off and . . .

Dance Two: Beginner Reel Step

Jump right 2-3, left 2-3, right 2-3, and left 2-3, right 2-3, left 2-3, right 2-3, left 2-3. (Lead out, students dance in a large circle around the floor. On the last 1-2-3 Ina yells out the next step to prepare the dancers for what is coming next.)

And (right) cut (to your knee) 2-3-4-5-6-7, (right) back 2-3, (left) back 2-3, (left) back 2-3-4-5-6-7, (left) back 2-3, (right) back 2-3.

Swing back and 1-2-3. (Lift right knee in front and swing it behind body and hit bum and then do a 1-2-3.)

Swing back and cut. (Lift left knee in front and swing it back behind body and hit bum and then do a 1-2-3.)

Right cut 2-3-4-5-6-7, swing back and 1-2-3.

Left swing back and 1-2-3, right swing back and cut.

Left cut 2-3-4-5-6-7, swing back and 1-2-3.

Right back 2-3, left back 2-3, right back 2-3-4-5-6-7 (head left).

Left back 2-3, right back 2-3, left back 2-3-4-5-6-7 (head right).

Right back 2-3, left back 2-3, right back 2-3-4-5-6-7.

Left back 2-3, right back 2-3, left back 2-3-4-5-6-7.

Lead around again to finish.

IF: OK, Aoife, you come out to the front and do it by yourself. Everyone else sit down and watch. Make sure to listen to the music—that is very important! [Aoife finishes and everyone claps.] Now stretch your leg as far as you can, do a nice point, no bump in the knee, cross the one leg in front of the other, and bow.

The rest of the beginner girls go one at a time. Ina addresses the problems each girl is having separately. She encourages each one to practice more during the week.

IF: OK now, we are going to do the other group's step. We need to make two lines. Everyone else come and sit down here [in front of the mirrors] and watch the other girls dance.

Dance Three: Advanced Beginner Reel Step

Lead out: 1-2-3-4-5-6-7, face front. (For the advanced beginners Ina does
not count out the 1-2-3s. Instead she assumes that the students can
handle that on their own.)
Back 2-3, back 2-3, cut 2-3-4-5-6-7.
Back 2-3, back 2-3, cut 2-3-4-5-6-7.
Swing hop back, swing hop back 1-2-3-4 (on your tippy toes).
Cut to knee for 1, turn 2-3-4-5-6-7. (Same sidestep we do in a line but this
time it is in a circle.)
Hopity hop (knee is up in front) and a 1-2-3.

IF: OK, now we'll go one at a time. No flat pancake feet! Up on your
                tippy toes. [Girls go one at a time.]

Dance Four: Basic Reel Step for Youngest Members of the Class

Lead around.
Cut 2-3-4-5-6-7, back 2-3, back 2-3.
Cut 2-3-4-5-6-7, back 2-3, back 2-3.
Hop hop 1-2-3, hop hop 1-2-3.
Back 2-3, back 2-3.
Back 2-3-4-5-6-7.
Hop hop 1-2-3, hop hop 1-2-3.
Back 2-3, back 2-3.
Back 2-3-4-5-6-7.

IF: OK, now, so those who know the South Kerry Set make your
                set. We are going to learn the second figure this week. [They had
                learned the first figure the previous week.]

Dance Five: South Kerry Set, Second Figure (Jigs: 152 bars)

House and square to home: each gent reverses his lady into the corner (in 2-3
and out 2-3) (two bars), and all house around to the place before their own
(six bars), gents facing out of the set at this point. Couples slide into the next
corner and quarter-turn clockwise, dancing 1-2-1, hop turn (two bars), slide
back to place (two bars), and turn once at home (four bars).

• Ina teaches them to house by counting "turning 1, turning 2, turning 3,
  turning 4, turning 5, and freeze, gents face out of the set."

• In order to remember which direction to go on the last bit she tells them to turn their elbows to home.

Top couples:
Slide and home: they dance into the set (two bars) and back (two bars), turn once at home (four bars), and repeat the whole movement.
House and square to home.
Top couples slide and home. (Slide in 1-2-3, slide out 1-2-3, turn 2-3, turn 2-3, turn 2-3, turn 2-3.)
House and square to home.
Side couples slide and home.
House and square to home.
Side couples slide and home.
House and square to home.

(Cahirciveen is located in South Kerry, so the students are learning a dance that originates in the area they are from.)

ADDITIONAL LESSON MATERIAL

Lesson Format for *Across the Water:*
Teaching Irish Music At Home and Abroad

Lesson:

Objective:

Goals:

Standards:

- Ireland Primary School Music Standards
- United States National Standards

Materials:

Transmission process:
1. Introducing the tradition
- Listen to music (guided listening).
- Learn about the history of the people.
- See pictures of instruments and musicians from the tradition.

2. Learning the tradition
- Learn songs (by rote).
- Dance.
- Learn to play tin whistle.

3. Experiencing the tradition
- Musicians are brought in to teach and play.
- Videos and DVDs are shown.

4. Discussing the tradition
- Teacher facilitates discussion around the topics of what was learned, questions students have as a result of this learning, and areas of further interest within the tradition.

5. Closing formulae

Assessment (continuous and noncontinuous)

Teacher reflection

Transcription of the Basic Milltown Jig Tune

Transcription of the Ornamented Milltown Jig

Tin Whistle Ornamentation Guide

The Cut

Musical symbol: ♪

Common use: It is a cut into the main note, which places emphasis on the main note.

Step 1: Begin by lifting the finger covering the second hole.

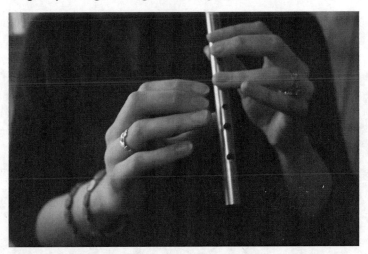

Step 2: Finger the main note, G.

Note: While completing a cut, the performer should not actually hear the auxiliary notes. Instead, it should sound like the main note, G, has been interrupted twice.

The Roll

Musical symbol: ⌣

Common use: In a jig, double rolls are used to ornament a note that is held for three beats. It is important to note that only the main note is tongued.

Step 1: Begin by playing the main note, which is G.

Step 2: Then lift the finger above the main note, which is A, while leaving the third finger down.

Step 3: Then play the main note again.

Step 4: Then finger the note below the main note, which is F'.

Step 5: Finally, return to the main note to complete the roll.

Short Roll

Musical symbol: ψ
Common use: In a jig, like the "Milltown Jig," the short roll is used to ornament a note that is held for two beats.

Step 1: Begin by fingering the note above the main note. Since in the "Milltown Jig" the main note is a G, an A would be played first.

Step 2: Then finger the main note, G.

Step 3: Next, finger the note below G, which is F'.

Step 4: Finally, return to the main note to complete the short roll.

Other Irish Traditional Music and Dance Resources

Books on Irish Music

Curtis, P. J. (1994). *Notes from the heart: A celebration of traditional Irish music.* Dublin: TORC.

Sawyers, J. S. (2000). *Celtic music: A complete guide.* Cambridge, MA: Da Capo Press.
Excellent resource on all Celtic music, from its beginnings to now. Great CD resources.

Woods, P. (1996). *The living note.* Dublin: O'Brien Press.

Irish Sheet Music

Healy, J. (1965). *Ballads from the pubs of Ireland: Popular songs and ballads* (vol. 1). Cork, Ireland: Ossian Publications.
This is a collection of forty-three complete songs with words, music, and chords.

Hughes, H. (1995). *Highlights edition Irish country songs.* New York: Boosey & Hawkes.
Traditional songs from various counties in Ireland.

Kennedy, P. (Ed.) (1975). *Folksongs of Britain and Ireland.* New York: Oak Publications.
These songs are in Gaelic and English. Each song is accompanied by an explanation of what it means and when it should be performed.

Leniston, F. (Ed.) (1992). *Popular Irish songs.* New York: Dover Publications.
This is a collection of thirty-six songs for voice and piano.

Maguire, T. (1996). *An Irish whistle tune book: 42 of the finest old Irish song-airs and a selection of lively traditional Irish dance tunes: Reels, jigs, hornpipes, slides, polkas, etc.* Cork, Ireland: Ossian Publications.
This book can be purchased with a demo tape.

O'Neill J. (1976). *More than 1,000 songs and dances of the Irish people.* New York: Hansen House. Shattinger International.

Dance Resources

Burchenal, E. (1924). *Rinnce na Eirann: National dances of Ireland.* New York: A. S. Barnes and Co.

Hammond, W. (1988). *Call the set: A guide to the dancing in the traditional style of two Munster sets.* Cork, Ireland: Cork Folk Publications.

Moylan, T. (1998). *Irish dances: A collection of ten traditional sets* (reprinted). Dublin: Na Piobairi Uilleann.

Quinn, T. (1997). *Irish dancing (Collins pocket reference).* Glasgow, UK: HarperCollins.

Irish Language and Folk Tale Resources

Curtain, J. (1975). *Myths and folklore of Ireland*. New York: Wing Books.
Danaher, K. (1998). *Folktales from the Irish countryside*. Dublin: Mercier Press.
Irish blessings with legends, poems & greetings. (1994). New York: Gramercy Books.
Reilly, C. A., & Reilly, R. T. (1999). *An Irish blessing: A photographic interpretation*. Notre Dame, IN: Sorin Books.
Wilkes, A. (2001). *Irish for beginners*. London: Usborne Publishing.
Yeats, W. B. (1993). *Irish fairy and folktales*. New York: Barnes & Noble.

Internet Resources

Ceolas Celtic music archive and other resources: www.ceolas.org/ceolas.html
International Comhaltas Ceoltóirí Éireann page: http://comhaltas.ie/
Ireland's main page: www.local.ie/
Irish Music Box—mp3 clips of traditional music: www.dojo.ie/musicbox/
Irish pronunciation: www.ultrasw.com/pawlowski/brendan/
Irish World Music Center, Limerick, Ireland: www.ul.ie/~iwmc/home.html
Rochester, NY, Comhaltas Ceoltóirí Éireann chapter: www.irishrochester.org

Discography

Graham, L., Ó Briain, G., & Uallacháin, P. (1999). *When I was young*. Dublin: Shanachie.

Heaney, J. (1996). *"Say a song" Joe Heaney in the Pacific Northwest: Irish songs in the old style (sean-nos)*. Seattle, WA: Northwest Folklife.

Uallachain, P. (2000). *Suantrai: An Irish lullaby*. Dublin: Shanachie Records.

Bibliography

Anderson, W. M., & Campbell, P. S. (1996). *Multicultural perspectives in music education* (2nd ed.). Reston, VA: MENC.

Blacking, J. (2000). *How musical is man?* Seattle: University of Washington Press.

Breathnach, B. (1996). *Folk music and dances of Ireland: A comprehensive study examining the basic elements of Irish folk music and dance traditions.* Cork, Ireland: Ossian Publications.

Campbell, P. S. (1991). *Lessons from the world: A cross-cultural guide to music teaching and learning.* New York: Schirmer Books.

Campbell, P. S., McCullough-Brabson, E., & Tucker, J. C. (1994). *Roots and branches: A legacy of multicultural music for children.* Danbury, CT: World Music Press.

Consortium of National Arts Education Associations (1994). *National standards for arts education.* Reston, VA: MENC.

Curtis, P. J. (1994). *Notes from the heart: A celebration of traditional Irish music.* Dublin: TORC.

Fleischmann, A. (1952). *Music in Ireland, a symposium.* Cork, Ireland: Cork University Press.

Gilmore, T. (1999). *Arts education curriculum.* Dublin: Government Publications Sales Office.

Hast, D. E., & Scott, S. (2004). *Music in Ireland: Experiencing music, expressing culture.* New York: Oxford University Press.

Kearns, T., & Taylor, B. (2003). *A Touchstone for the tradition: The Willie Clancy summer school.* Dingle, Ireland: Brandon, 7–8.

Leyden, M. (1989). *Belfast: City of song.* Dingle, Ireland: Brandon.

Lundquist, B., & Szego, C. K. (1998). *Musics of the world's cultures: A source book for music educators.* Reading, UK: Callaway International Resource Center for Music Education.

Mac Aoidh, C. (1996). The critical role of education in the development of tradi-
    tional music in the republic of Ireland. In F. Vallely, H. Hamilton, E. Vallely &
    L. Doherty (Eds.), *Crosbhealach an cheoil—the crossroads conference*. Dublin:
    Ossian Publications.
McCarthy, M. (1999). *Passing it on: The transmission of music in Irish culture*. Cork,
    Ireland: Cork University Press.
Mc Mahon, T. (1996). Music of the powerful and majestic past. In F. Vallely, H.
    Hamilton, E. Vallely & L. Doherty (Eds.), *Crosbhealach an cheoil—the crossroads
    conference*. Dublin: Ossian Publications.
Merriam-Webster online dictionary (2009). Springfield, MA: Merriam-Webster Inc.
    Retrieved from www.m-w.com.
Moulden, J. (1996). Sing us a folk song mouldy. In F. Vallely, H. Hamilton, E. Val-
    lely & L. Doherty (Eds.), *Crosbhealach an cheoil—the crossroads conference*.
    Dublin: Ossian Publications.
Nettl, B. (1995). *Heartland excursions: Ethnomusicological reflections on schools of
    music*. Urbana: University of Illinois Press.
Nettl, B. (1998). An ethnomusicological perspective. In B. Lundquist & C. K. Szego
    (Eds.), *Music of the world's cultures: A source book for music educators*. Reading,
    UK: Callaway International Resource Center for Music Education.
Nettl, B., Capwell, C., Bohlman, P. V., Wong, I. K. F., & Turino, T. (2003). *Excur-
    sions in world music* (4th ed.). Upper Saddle River, NJ: Pearson Education.
O Canainn, T. (1993). *Traditional music in Ireland*. Cork: Ossian Publications.
Pine, R. (1998). Music in Ireland 1848–1998: An overview. In *Music in Ireland
    1848–1998*. Boulder, CO: Mercier Press.
Sawyers, J. S. (2000). *Celtic music: A complete guide*. Cambridge, MA: Da Capo
    Press.
Shields, H., & Gershen, P. (2000). Ireland. In *Garland encyclopedia of world music:
    Europe*. New York: Garland Publishing, 378–391.
Smith, T. (1996). The challenge of bringing oral traditions of music into an academic
    teaching environment. In F. Vallely, H. Hamilton, E. Vallely & L. Doherty (Eds.),
    Crosbhealach an cheoil—the crossroads conference. Dublin: Ossian Publications.
Titon, J. T. (1996). *Worlds of music: An introduction to the music of the world's
    peoples*. New York, NY: Schirmer Books.
Vallely, F. (1999). *The companion to Irish traditional music*. Cork: Cork University
    Press.
Woods, P. (1996). *The living note*. Dublin: O'Brien Press.

About the Author

Rebecca E. Farrell is currently the lead teacher for the art and music departments at Palmyra-Macedon Central School District, Palmyra, New York, and an elementary general and choral music teacher. She has spent most of her adult life learning and studying Irish traditional music and dance. She is a member of the Young School of Irish Dance and the Tom Finucane Branch of the Comhaltas Ceoltóirí Éireann (CCE). An active member of the CCE, she has taught numerous workshops on Irish music and travel, leads a monthly singing session in Rochester, and is featured as a vocal soloist on the CCE CD titled *Irish Rochester.*

She has a master's degree in music education from Ithaca College in Ithaca, New York, and a master's degree in ethnomusicology from the University of Limerick in Limerick, Ireland. She lives in Rochester, New York, with her husband, Brian, and their cats, Homie and Zira.